Péter Mujzer

History of The 40/43M Zrínyi Assault Howitzer

KAGERO publishing

inCOMBAT

History of the 40/43M Zrínyi Assault Howitzer • Péter Mujzer

First edition • LUBLIN 2021

Photo credits: **Bonhardt Attila, Deák Tamás, ECPA, Éder Miklós, Fortepan, Illésfalvi Péter, Karai Sándor, Mujzer Péter, Pálinkás Zsolt, Sárhidai Gyula, Szollár János, Kovácsházy Miklós, War Correspondent Company**

Coloured photos: **Deák Tamás**

Drawings: **Bíró Ádám, Bajtos Iván**

Cover: **Arkadiusz Wróbel**

Colour profiles: **Arkadiusz Wróbel**

DTP: **KAGERO STUDIO**

ISBN: 978-83-66673-37-3

Printed in Poland

KAGERO Publishing • e-mail: kagero@kagero.pl, marketing@kagero.pl
Editorial office, Marketing, Distribution: KAGERO Publishing,
Akacjowa 100, os. Borek – Turka, 20-258 Lublin 62, Poland, phone/fax +48 81 501 21 05

www.kagero.pl • shop.kagero.pl

Table of Contents

INTRODUCTION

The lessons learned from the ongoing war already proved the combat value of the self-propelled/assault artillery as early as 1941. The Hungarian troops wanted self-propelled artillery, anti-tank and anti-aircraft vehicles as early as 1940. The cavalry troops had a 75mm horse-drawn mountain gun battery on a regimental level. The infantry regiments of the 2nd Hungarian Army were reinforced with horsed drawn escort batteries with aged 80mm light guns. However, these elements were far away from what the requirements of the modern war requested and the Army was aware of it.

The Hungarian Ministry of Defence recommended the organization of the self-propelled artillery in 1942. By the end of 1943, the organization of the two Hungarian armored divisions completed. The next step was to organize and equipped the assault artillery. The theoretical guidelines, methodology, and practice had been learned from the Germans. The Hungarian Army Command wanted to purchase German assault guns but the German side has blocked the sale of their proven assault guns or their production right since 1942.

Captain József Barankay the founder of the Hungarian Assault Artillery Branch and the first commander of the 1st Assault Artillery Battalion in 1944. [Kovácsházy]

DESIGN AND PRODUCTION

The Hungarian military leadership, therefore, commissioned the Weiss Manfred Factory (WM) to design and manufacture a new self-propelled artillery vehicle. General Major Árpád Denk-Doroszlay (Chief of Logistic) and Jurgen János, Chief Engineer (WM's Technical Director) agreed that the new assault artillery vehicle will be built on the already available main parts of the Turán tank already in production and the available 40M 105mm howitzer and the 43M 75mm

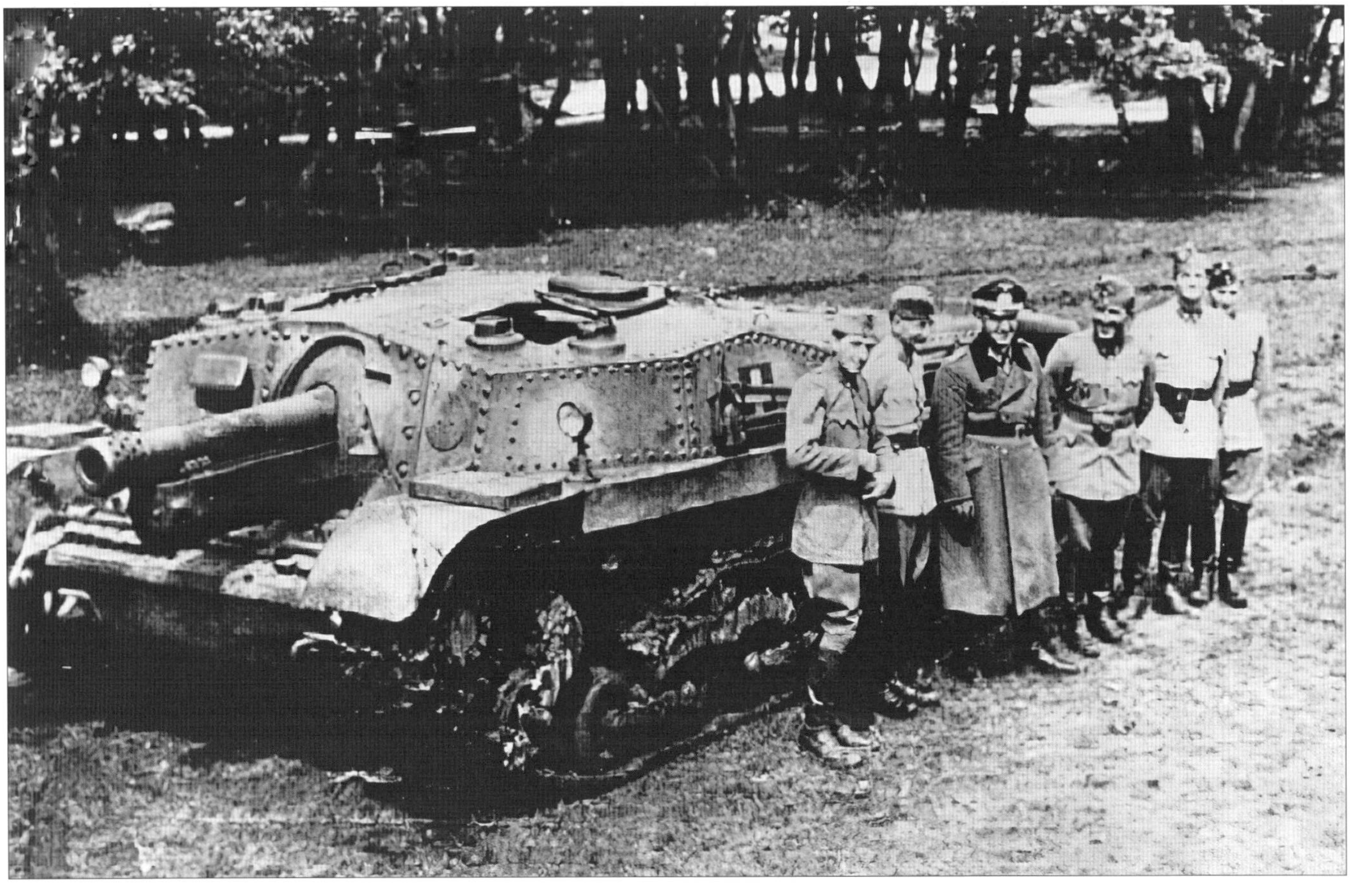

The 40/43M Zrínyi assault howitzer with the German artillery officer Lieutenant Colonel Balthasar sided by 1st Lieutenants Gábor Becsey, Ernő Gömbös and Captain József Barankay and 1st Lieutenants Fedor Wáczek, Béla Guthy in September 1943. [Kovácsházy]

long-barreled gun. Based on the discussions, the final plans were prepared by Ernő Kovácsházy, a mechanical engineer (the chief engineer of the tank division at WM).

According to unconfirmed sources, Hungarian experts visited Italy somewhere 1941-42, where they were shown around the factory where Semovente assault guns were produced for the Italian Army. The Italian Semovente self-propelled gun was designed on the basis of the Italian M13/40 medium tank in 1941. There is no proofed evidence whether the Hungarians were influenced by their Italian colleges. At least we can say that the concept of the Italian and Hungarian design was very similar.

DESIGN OF THE ASSAULT ARTILLERY VEHICLE

The Turán tank turret was removed; the chassis was widened to 40 cm in width, to install and handle the gun. The gun is placed behind the 75 mm thick, thickened, frontal armor plate. The fighting compartment was a spacious box with wide, polygonal, tilted armor plates (25-13 mm).

The hull was made in riveted and bolted version as the Turán family. The length of the Zrínyi body, the driven chain elements, the power transmission systems, the controls, and the suspension, as well as the production technology, remained the same as Turán tanks.

The already well-proven 43M rotatable periscope was installed on the roof slides and hatches, and an escape hatch was built on the underside of the vehicle. Widening the body has improved the maneuverability of the vehicle. The fuel tank's capacity reached 445 liters, so the vehicle's range - on road - increased to 280 km.

The Zrínyi assault howitzer based on the 40/41M Turán tanks, this 40M Turán medium tank was knocked out at the bridgehead of Szentes, belonged to the 1st Tank Regiment. [Bartus]

The 41M Turán heavy tank was the heaviest Hungarian made tanks during the war but was ineffective with its short barrel 75mm gun, the Zrínyi project aimed to provide heavier punch against the Soviet medium/heavy tanks. (Fortepan, Lissák)

The Hungarian border guard, mountain battalions and the hussar regiments had close support pack/horsed drawn 15/31M 75mm mountain gun batteries. [Mujzer]

The 260 horsepower 4-stroke, water-cooled, 8-cylinder Turán petrol engine could move the 21.6 tons (with skirt plates) vehicle at a maximum speed of 43 km/h.

The Zrínyi had the gearbox of the Túrán tank, with compressed air, six forward and six reverse gears, and equipped with steering wheel brakes. Driving the vehicle was simple: the driver pulled the lever in the direction of rotation by breaking the side chain.

When the lever was fully pulled, the Zrínyi could turn around on the spot. The vehicle was able to move along a 45° slope in good terrain with good lateral stability. The braking distance was then 200-250 m.

The 40/43M Zrínyi assault howitzer's full length was 5500 mm, the barrel was 5900 mm, and the armored body itself was 5100 mm long. The width of the vehicle is 2890 mm; its height is 1900 mm without the periscope.

The lower front panel closed the hull, which was also equipped with 1-1 drawbar hooks. Mudguards were mounted above the chassis, which slid backward at 3°. The headlights are positioned on the edge of the mudguard. The fire extinguisher was positioned behind the left headlamp and on the right side, the loudspeaker of the horn was attached. On the inside of the front mudguards, there were additional tools; the left-side was a wire cutter, on the right side a special tool for replacing the track, and a hammer for bolt pinching. In front of the headlamps, 2-2 thick wooden blocks for lifting were secured.

The armored hull was joined by the superstructure, the sidewalls of which were tilted 80 degrees inwards. Additional hand tools were secured to the superstructure; to the left, a field shovel, jimmy, pickaxe, and a large hammer for mud shedding, a steel tow cable to the right. In the lower part of the engine compartment, there is a bullet-proof grille that can be locked from inside with 4-4 shuttering louvers. On the sloping front panel, there is a circular mounting window for maintenance purposes and there are two iron straps that clamp the replacement track parts. The drivers' observation panel is located on the frontal armor plate, right to the gun. This was also different on the iron sample vehicle, the first three vehicles in the series, and the other serial produced vehicles.

The infantry regiments of the 2nd Hungarian Army were reinforced with escort batteries of 80mm 5/8M light field guns, totally inadequate in 1942. [War Correspondent Company/WCC]

The 1st Armoured Field Division got a few Marder tank hunter vehicles in January 1943. The vehicle's long barrel 75mm gun could knock out the Soviet medium and heavy tanks. [Fortepan]

The 1st Independent Tank Hunter Company was equipped with the Marders in January 1943, fought well during the retreat; the only surviving vehicle was given back to the Germans. [ECPA]

The Hungarian Assault Artillery got about 40 StuG. III assault gun in autumn of 1944, served at the 7th Assault Artillery Battalion. [Mujzer]

Late 1944, Hetzer 38[t] tank hunters were also provided to the Hungarians, this knocked out Hetzer belonged to the 20th Assault Gun Battalion, tactical number T-038.

The H-801 iron vehicle was equipped with a one-one round-shaped observation aperture for the driver and the gun layer. The first three Zrínyi II (3H-000-3H-002) of the series were equipped with the driver observation panel of the 41M Turán tank. In the other vehicles of the series, this round-shape plate in front of the gun layer was completely gone, and the driver got the new 10-cm-higher 43M driver's observation panel.

In the center of the frontal armor plate, slid by 150 mm from the longitudinal axis to left, was fitted a hinged locking sphere to move the gun, formally known as an armor spherical ball. This was protected by the gun shield attached to the front panel.

Zrínyi's armament was a 105mm howitzer, or a 75mm anti-tank gun and a light machine gun; finally excluded from the weaponry.

The ammunition allowance was 52 rounds per vehicle. According to the battlefield experiences, the crew could pack more than 30 rounds at the expense of the individual equipment. The ammunition allowance consisted of 38/33M

Hungarian Hetzer 38[t] tank hunter vehicle abandoned in early 1945, its tactical number 033.

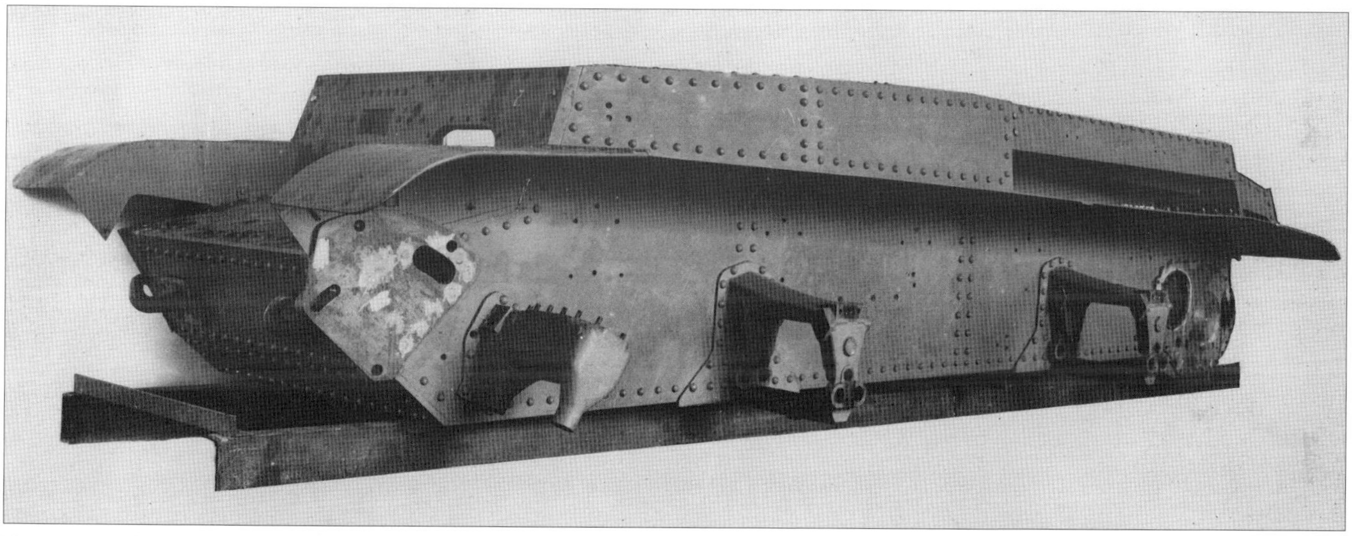

The armoured hull of the Zrínyi assault vehicles based on the chassis of the Turán tanks, but it was widened to accommodate the artillery pieces, which gave more stability to the new vehicle. [Service Manual]

The 40/43M Zrínyi II assault howitzer was armed with the 40M 105mm field howitzer, produced by the MÁVAG Ordnance Factory at Diósgyőr. It was a stopgap solution but worked well. [Sárhidai]

The iron prototype of the 40/43M Zrínyi, number plate H-801 with the identical oval shape visor slot of the gunner. [Bonhardt]

HE-fragmentation, 42M HEAT, and 38/33M smoke shells. The assault howitzer fired cased separate loading ammunition, made the rate of fire slower, only 5 to 6 shots per minute.

The crew was armed for close protection with four service pistols, three sub-machineguns, eight hand grenades, and one flare pistol. These were placed inside the assault howitzer.

The firing of the gun may have occurred with compressed air or mechanically. Its vertical angle of travel was -5° - + 25° vertical, 11°-11° horizontally. The Zrínyit was designed with a targeting device designed to fire with direct and shared sight. The latter had never been used in combat.

The R5/a type radio was installed in the vehicle. The crew (commander, gun layer, loader-radio operator, and the driver)

The iron prototype 40/43M Zrínyi assault howitzer, commanded by 1st Lieutenant Dénes Sándor, the vehicles had the identical double megaphone of the horn. [Bonhardt]

The prototype, iron vehicle of the 40/43M Zrínyi assault howitzer H-801 with the identical oval shape visor slots for the driver and the gunner on the frontal armoured plate. Later it was replaced by the normal driver visor apparatus, the gunner's slot disappeared. [Bonhardt]

Resting crew of the 40/43M Zrínyi assault howitzer at Hajmáskér training area, the fire extinguisher and the entrenching tools are visible on the left side of the hull. [Bonhardt]

wore the 39M Italian style crash helmet with a well-insulated headset and mechanic overalls in the vehicle. The commander directed the vehicle's main armament (howitzer) by commands by the intercom or due to the combat noise with conventional signals or sounding horn. The gun layer also could signal with green and red light signals to the driver to adjust the rough direction of the gun.

PRODUCTION

The Ministry of Defence ordered 40 assault howitzers in January 1943. Later 50 plus assault howitzer was ordered. The fighting ability of the Turán could not be improved so the plan was to mass-produce the assault howitzers. To combat the Soviet T-34 tank, it was decided to produce an assault gun with a 75mm gun on the same chassis, named the Zrínyi I assault gun. The first assault gun battalion was set up and equipped with 34 Zrínyis in March 1944, but 40/43. M Zrínyi II production was slow. The Zrínyi I prototype was finished in February 1944, but the long-barrelled gun had some problems which were not possible to solve. Only the prototype of the assault gun was finished.

On 27 July 1944, Allied air raids struck the Weiss Manfred Factory and ended the mass production of the assault howitzers. About 15-20 half-finished vehicles and spare parts were salvaged from the destroyed Factory. The last Zrínyi assault howitzers were completed at Ganz Factory in September-October 1944. Even some of the Zrínyis went to the front line directly from the factory until the end of 1944. The last known numberplate was 3H-066, the Weiss Manfred Factory produced 66 Zrínyi assault howitzers until 27 July 1944. The Ganz Factory assembled 10 vehicles until the end of 1944. All in all, about 76 Zrínyi assault howitzers were produced.

The HTI made efforts to reinforce the firepower of the Zrínyi assault howitzers using the German Nebelwerfer rocket launchers in late 1943, early 1944. The original Nebelwerfer rocket launcher had six 15cm rocket tubes already used by the Hungarian Army, it was divided into two packs of three rocket tubes and was attached to each rear side of the hull.

40/43 M Zrínyi assault howitzer, number plate 3H-024 during a winter exercise in early 1944, the vehicle already belonged to the 1st Assault Artillery Battalion. [Bonhardt]

Battery commander sitting in his position with open hatches, the 1st Lieutenant wearing the 39M crash helmet with intercom, the inner side of the armoured hatches were padded to protect the crew. [Kovácsházy]

Resting crew around the 40/43M Zrínyi assault howitzer, wearing the mechanic overalls and field caps, belonging to the Assault Artillery Training Cadre Unit at Hajmáskér in 1943-1944. Behind the assault, the howitzer is a Turán tank visible. [Bonhardt]

Gun commander leading his vehicles in open hatch position, wearing the 39M crash helmets with intercom. This 40/43M Zrínyi assault howitzer was the prototype H-801, had stick antenna for the radio. [Bonhardt]

40/43M Zrínyi assault howitzer during the training at Hajmáskér. On the left side of the vehicle next to the fire extinguisher are the entrenching tools, axe, hammer and spade attached to the hull. [Kovácsházy]

40/43M Zrínyi assault howitzer on firing exercise at Hajkmáskér training area. At the back of the vehicle attached the toolbox, five smoke candles and one the spare roller. [Bonhardt]

A close photo of the smoke candle canisters on the back of a Turán tank, similar to the Zrínyi assault howitzer. Some of the canisters are open, the smoke candles operated by the crew from the vehicle. [Bonhardt]

Hungarian 40/43M Zrínyi assault howitzer at Vác, December 1944. The back of the vehicle is well visible with the two jacks on the engine deck, the toolbox, five smoke candles and spare roller attached to the back of the Zrínyi, the towing cables attached to the right side of the hull. [Karai]

The concept was to use the rocket fire to annihilate the enemy's anti-tank position in time before the Zrínyis reach the killing zone of the anti-tank gun. The practical range of the rockets was about 2000-7000 meters. In theory, a fire strike of six 15cm Nebelwerfer rockets could destroy a whole anti-tank battery by hitting the identified position of the enemy.

40/43M Zrínyi assault howitzer during the training at Hajmáskér in spring of 1944. The complicated running gear system of the Turán tanks was used on the Zrínyis too. [Kovácsházy]

The 40/43M Zrínyi assault howitzer used the barrel of the 40M light field howitzer, firing the divided ammunition which reduced the rate of fire of the Zrínyi assault howitzer too. The typical short, spent shell cases can be seen around the assault howitzer during the firing exercise. [Bonhardt]

TECHNICAL DATA

Designation: **40/43M Zrínyi II (Zrínyi 105) assault howitzer**
Years of production: 1942-1944
Factory/produces quantity: Weis Manfred Factory/ 66 – Ganz Factory/10
Combat weight: 21,50 t – 22,5 t with skirt plates
Length: 5900 mm (with the gun)
Width: 2890 mm
Height: 1900 mm
Ground pressure: 0,75 kp/cm^2
Crew: 4
Engine: Manfred Weiss V8
Displacement: 14866 cm^3
Cylinders: 8
Horsepower: 260 Hp
Speed: 43 km/h – 40 km/h with skirt plates
Range: 220 km on the road
Obstacles:
– steps: 0,8 m
– ditch: 2,2 m
– ford: 0,9 m
Armament: one 40. M 105 mm L/20 howitzer
range: 10,500 m
rate of fire: 6 shots/minute
Ammunition: 52 shells (30 fragmentation, 16 armoured piercing, 6 smoke)
Armor: 13-75mm
Radio: one R-5/a radio with stick antenna

Running gear system of the Zrínyi assault artillery vehicles were identical to the Turán tanks, the complicated gear system was vulnerable and could easily clog with the earth. [Bonhardt]

The right side view of the running gear with driven sprocket, running rollers and tension wheel and leaf springs are visible. [Bonhardt]

Designation: **44M Zrínyi I (Zrínyi 75) assault gun**
Years of production: 1944
Factory/produced quantity: Weis Manfred Factory/ one prototype
Combat weight: 22 t
Length: 7350 mm with gun
Width: 2890 mm
Height: 1900 mm
Ground pressure: 0,72 kp/cm^2
Crew: 4
Engine: Manfred Weiss V8-4
Displacement: 14866 cm^3
Cylinders: 8
Horsepower: 260 Hp
Speed: 43km/h - 40 km/h with skirt plates
Range: 220 km on the road
Obstacles:
– step: 0,8 m
– ditch: 2,2 m
– ford: 0,9 m
Armament: one 43. M 75mm L55 gun
rate of fire: 12 rounds/minute
Armour: 13-75 mm
Radio: one R-5/a radio with stick antenna

Two pairs of towing hooks were situated at the front and rear side of the chassis, the towing cables were attached to the right side of the hull. [Bonhardt]

The 8/14M artillery sight for indirect fire installed on the 40/43M Zrínyi assault howitzer, it was practically never used, because the assault artillery fired direct shots. [Bonhardt]

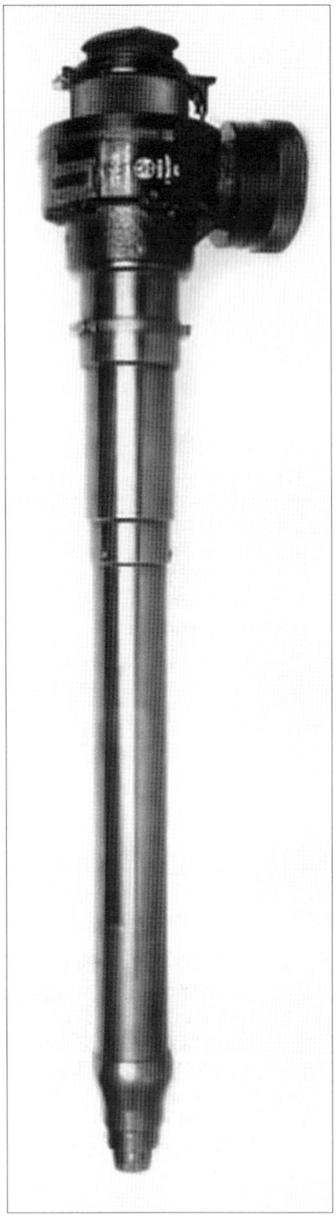

LEFT PICTURE: 43M gun sight for the 105mm assault howitzer. [Service manual]

RIGHT PICTURE: 43M periscope for the 40/43M Zrínyi assault howitzer. [Service Manual]

The driver of the 40/43M Zrínyi assault howitzer sitting on an adjustable seat at his driver position. [Service Manual]

ORGANISATION

ASSAULT ARTILLERY BRANCH

In December 1942, two Hungarian officers traveled to Jütebog (near Berlin) for further training in the assault artillery school. One of the two was Captain József Barankay. At the same time groups of 40 Hungarian officers received German artillery retraining. The first assault artillery cadre unit started to form on 1 March 1943.

On 3 July 1943, the first officer training course for assault artillery officers started. From a high number of volunteers, only the most distinguished officers were selected by Captain Barankay.

17 May 1944 the Minister of Defence had been adapted the Command of the Assault Artillery Training Camp at Hajmáskér. The authority of the Command included the integrated training of the assault artillery units, leadership, reserve officer training, cooperated exercises, gunnery, organization, and recommendation for modernization. Major-General Ernő Billnitzer, a field artillery officer had become the head of the new artillery branch until the end of the war. He had under his command eight assault artillery battalions, training, and replacement units.

Assault artillery crew gathering around their 40/43M Zrínyi assault howitzer wearing their mechanic overall at Hajmáskér Assault Artillery Training Cadre in 1944. The vehicle has the late style of military insignia. [Deák]

The gun commanders directed their vehicles with open hatches, which made them vulnerable to enemy small arms fire too. The vehicle had the late style white cross in black square military insignia. [Kovácsházy]

40/43M Zrínyi assault howitzer during the cooperation exercise with infantry in summer of 1944 at Hajmáskér training ground. The crew dressed in mechanic overall. [Bonhardt]

40/43M Zrínyi assault howitzer during the obstacle course at Hajmáskér in 1944. The assault howitzer could climb a 0.8meter step. [Bonhardt]

Breechblock of the 75mm gun of the 44M Zrínyi I assault gun, just one prototype was completed based on the iron version of the Zrínyi vehicles. [Service manual]

Experimental 44M Zrinyi I assault gun armed with 75mm Pak 40 anti-tank gun, behind the assault gun is the 40/43M Zrínyi II assault howitzer at the yard of the Ordnance Depot. [Sárhidai]

Frontal view of the 44M Zrínyi I assault gun, originally the assault artillery battalions would consist of two assault gun and one assault howitzer batteries. [Deák]

The final upgrade of the Zrínyi I assault gun was the added 150mm rocket launchers tubes attached to both sides of the hull. [Bonhardt]

Factory test trial of the first three serial vehicles of the 40/43M Zrínyi assault howitzers in 1943, the assault howitzers had the Tuán style driver visor, the KÁB stands for Military Acceptance Committee. The guns covered with canvas protective cover. [Bonhardt]

On 1 August 1943, after the completion of the conversation course, the 1st Hungarian Royal Honvéd Assault Artillery Battalion was formed at Hajmáskér, commanded by Captain Barankay. In the beginning, the assault artillerymen had used Turán and Toldi tanks for training. The first three assault howitzers arrived in September 1943, license plate numbers were: 3H-000, 3H-001, 3 H-002. The training had started with Toldi and Turán tanks. The 1st Assault Gun Battalion had ten-ten 41M heavy Turán and 38. M Toldi light tanks, and each of the 2nd- 8th Assault Gun Training Cadres received seven heavy 41M Turán heavy tanks.

The mass production of the Turán and Zrínyi vehicles ended by the Allied air raids on 27 July 1944. The salvaged parts and components were used to build additional vehicles. [Bonhardt]

Armoured hulls of the never completed 40/43M Zrínyi assault howitzers, at the GANZ Factory in spring of 1945. These were scrapped as all of the Hungarian armoured vehicles after the war. [Sárhidai]

Assault artillery officer training held by Captain József Barankay, dressed in mechanic overalls. Volunteered field artillery officers were selected for the training. [Kovácsházy]

Assault artillerymen with their early production 40/43M Zrínyi assault howitzer with the Turán style driver slot, at the yard of the Assault Artillery Training Cadre at Hajmáskér in summer of 1944. [Deák]

Young Sergeants, gun commanders posing on the barrel of the early production 40/43M assault howitzer in front of the garage at Hajmáskér. [Deák]

Members of the first Assault Artillery Officer's Training Course lined in front of the garage at Hajmáskér. The first officer from the left is 1st Lieutenant Ernő Gömbös. [Kovácsházy]

Assault Artillery Training Cadres started the training with 41M Turán heavy tanks; the 40/43M Zrínyi assault howitzer had the unit sign of the 3rd Battery of the 1st Assault Artillery Battalion in spring of 1944. [Mujzer]

Signal training at the Assault Artillery Officer's Training Course, the officer on the left is Lieutenant Barnabás Kőszeghy, later commanded the 1/7 Assault Artillery Battery. [Kovácsházy]

Curious reserve officers gathered around a 40/43M Zrínyi assault howitzer during a summer exercise in 1944. Theoretically, the assault artillery was subordinated to the infantry divisions providing close artillery support to the subordinated divisional units. [Deák]

Late serial production 40/43M Zrínyi assault howitzer with 43M driver's visor slot at Hajmáskér in late 1943 with white cross military insignia. [Bonhardt]

40/43 M Zrínyi assault howitzer, belonged to the first three series produced assault howitzers, with a double megaphone and new 43M driver's slot, parking at the yard of Hajmáskér. [Deák]

Attacking 40/43M Zrínyi assault howitzer on the Hajmáskér Training Field, the vehicle still had the Turán driver's visor apparatus, the low profiles help it to hide and camouflage. [Bonhardt]

Young ensign at the driver's position of the 40/43M Zrínyi assault howitzer. The vehicles belonged to the first three assault howitzer produced by the Hungarians; already replaced 43M visor apparatus for the driver. [Deák]

ORGANIZATIONAL STRUCTURE

Theoretically, each Army Corps had an assault artillery battalion, which was directly subordinated to the Corps, and could be assigned to support any division of the corps.

An assault artillery battalion organically consisted of:

– Battalion commander (one assault gun).

– Staff battery with motorized sapper, signal, maintenance, medical and motorcycle platoons, pus supply column

Painted by/Rysował: Arkadiusz Wróbel

The prototype of the 40/43M Zrínyi assault howitzer with three tone camouflage at Hajmáskér artillery training field, evaluation course in 1943, without military insignia.

40/43M Zrínyi assault howitzer with three tones camouflage (dark brown, olive green, sand yellow) with the late style military insignia, white cross in black square.

Painted by/Rysował: Arkadiusz Wróbel

40/43M Zrínyi assault howitzer belonged to the 3. Battery of the 1. Assault Gun Battalion deployed to Galicia, summer of 1944. The Zrínyi wears the olive green standard camouflage with late style military insignia, and big white tactical number 32, refers to the 2. vehicle of the 3. Battery.

40/43M Zrínyi assault howitzer belonged to the 3. Battery of the 1. Assault Gun Battalion, in Galicia, summer of 1944. The Zrínyi has the three tones camouflage, white tactical number, without military insignia. The protection of the assault howitzers were upgraded on the front line with perforated skirts.

Painted by/Rysował: Arkadiusz Wróbel

40/43M Zrínyi assault howitzer 1. Battery of the 1. Assault Artillery Battalion, the skirt plated vehicle painted dark olivegreen, with big tactical number and a big white cross military insignia.

40/43M Zrínyi assault howitzer belonged to the 3. Battery of the 1. Assault Artillery Battalion, April of 1944, during the deployement to Galícia. The Zrínyi had a two digit tactical number and the military insignia painted on the side of the vehicle.

Metal Assault Artillery Branch sign worn on the uniform or on the side of the field cap with red colour artillery fabric washer. [Deák]

Original photo of the 40/43M Zrínyi assault howitzer with the divided ammunitions. [Bonhardt]

Coloured photo of a 40/43M Zrínyi assault howitzer on firing exercise. [Deák]

Coloured photo of a 40/43M Zrínyi assault howitzer on training, it had a low profile an advantage in combat. [Deák]

Coloured photo of a 40/43M Zrínyi assault howitzer painted in dark olive-green camouflage. [Deák]

Coloured photo of a 40/43M Zrínyi assault howitzer with skirt plate and tracks added to the hull. The large size white cross military insignia painted on the skirt plate too. [Deák]

Coloured photo of the prototype of the 40/43M Zrínyi assault howitzer on the field trial. [Deák]

Coloured photo of a 40/43M Zrínyi assault howitzer on an obstacle course at Hajmáskér. [Deák]

Original colour photo of a 40/43M Zrínyi assault howitzer painted in three colour camouflage. [Bonhardt]

Original colour photo of a 40/43M Zrínyi assault howitzer painted in three colour camouflage. [Bonhardt]

Original colour photo of the frontal view of of the 40/43M Zrínyi assault howitzer in 1943 at Hajmáskér. [Bonhardt]

Coloured photo of the prototype of the 40/43M Zrínyi assault howitzer at Hajmáskér. [Deák]

Coloured photo of a damaged 40/43M Zrínyi assault howitzer belonged to the 10th Assault Howitzer Battalion, autumn of 1944, Transylvania. [Deák]

Coloured photo of a 40/43M Zrínyi assault howitzer blown up due to internal explosion at Kelenföld / Budapest summer of 1945. [Deák]

Unit sign of the 2nd Assault Howitzer Battery/ 1st Assault Artillery Battalion painted on the frontal mudguard and the back of the vehicle.

Unit sign of the 3rd Assault Howitzer Battery/ 1st Assault Artillery Battalion painted on the frontal mudguard and the back of the vehicle.

Tactical numbering painted on the side skirt plate, belonged to the 3rd Battery/1st Assault Artillery Battalion, spring 1944. [Deák]

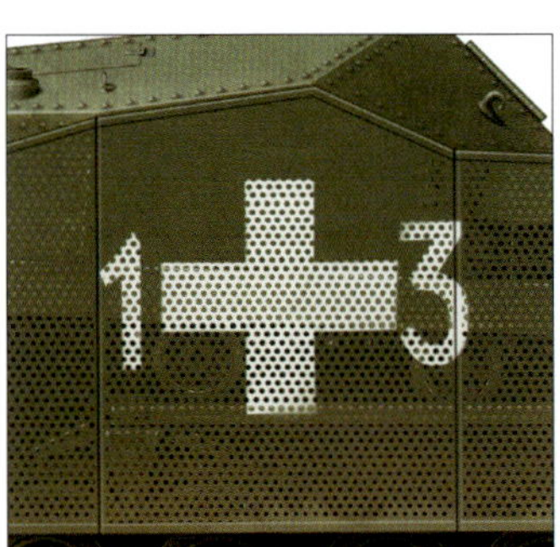

Modified military insignia and tactical number painted on the side skirt plate of the 1st Assault Artillery battalion in summer of 1944, Galicia. [Deák]

Small tactical number painted on the three tone camouflaged skirt plate of the Zrínyi assault howitzer belonged to the 3rd Battery/1st Assault Artillery Battalion, spring 1944. [Deák]

Large scale military insignia painted on the engine deck of the Zrínyi assault howitzer in summer of 1944. [Deák]

Side view of the 40/43M Zrínyi II assault howitzer [Bajtos]

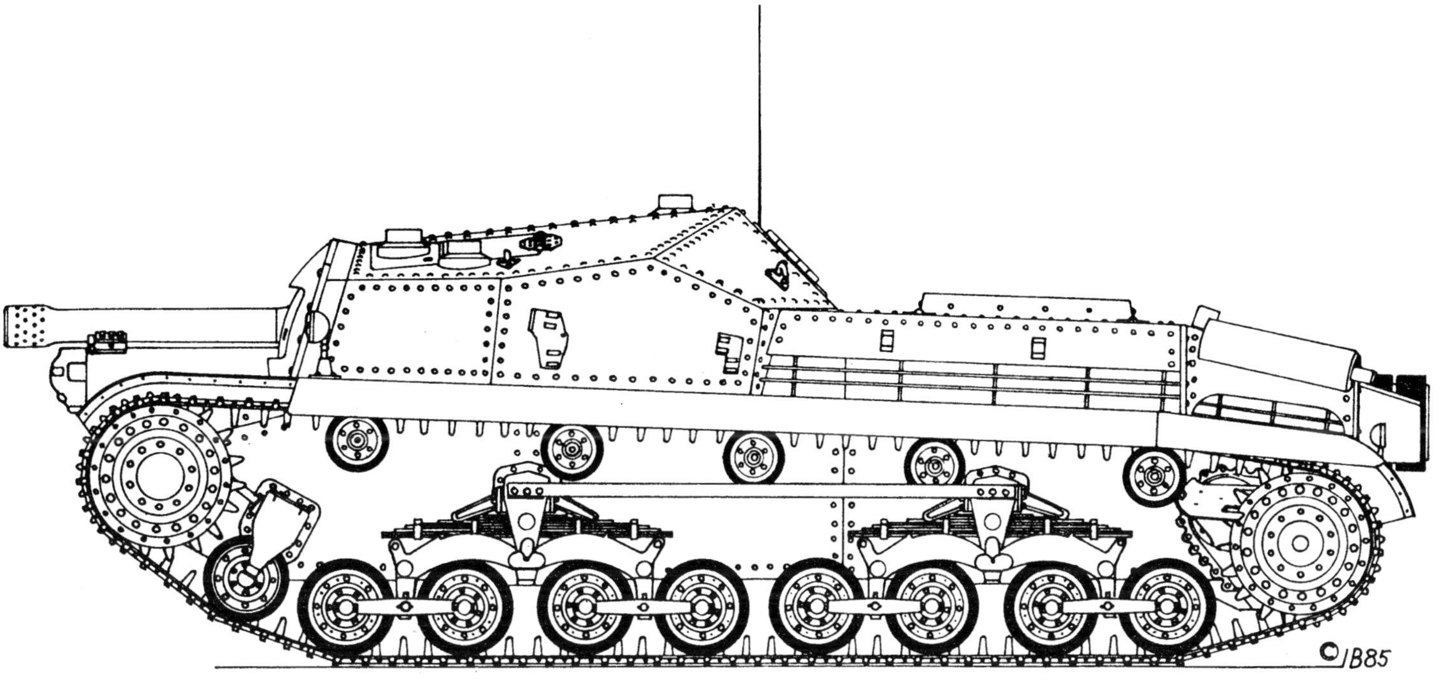

Four views of the 40/43M Zrínyi II assault howitzer [Bajtos]

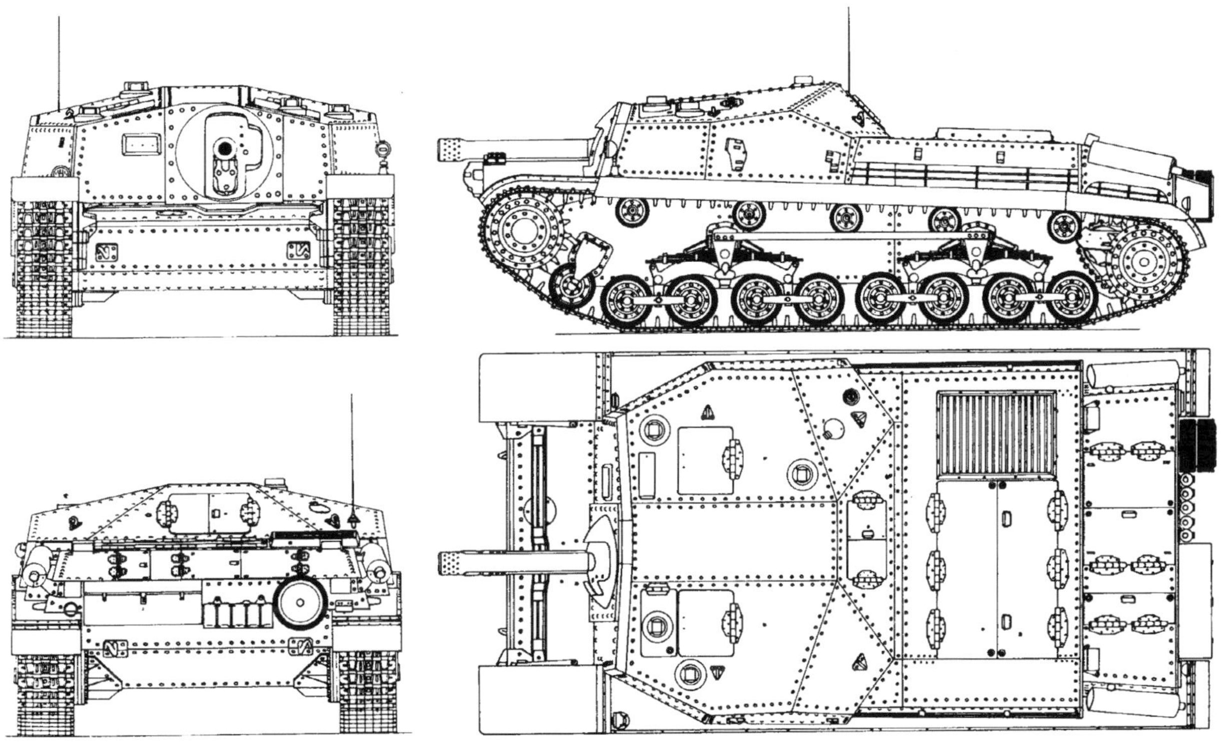

Frontal and back views of the prototype of the 44M Zrínyi I assault gun [Bajtos]

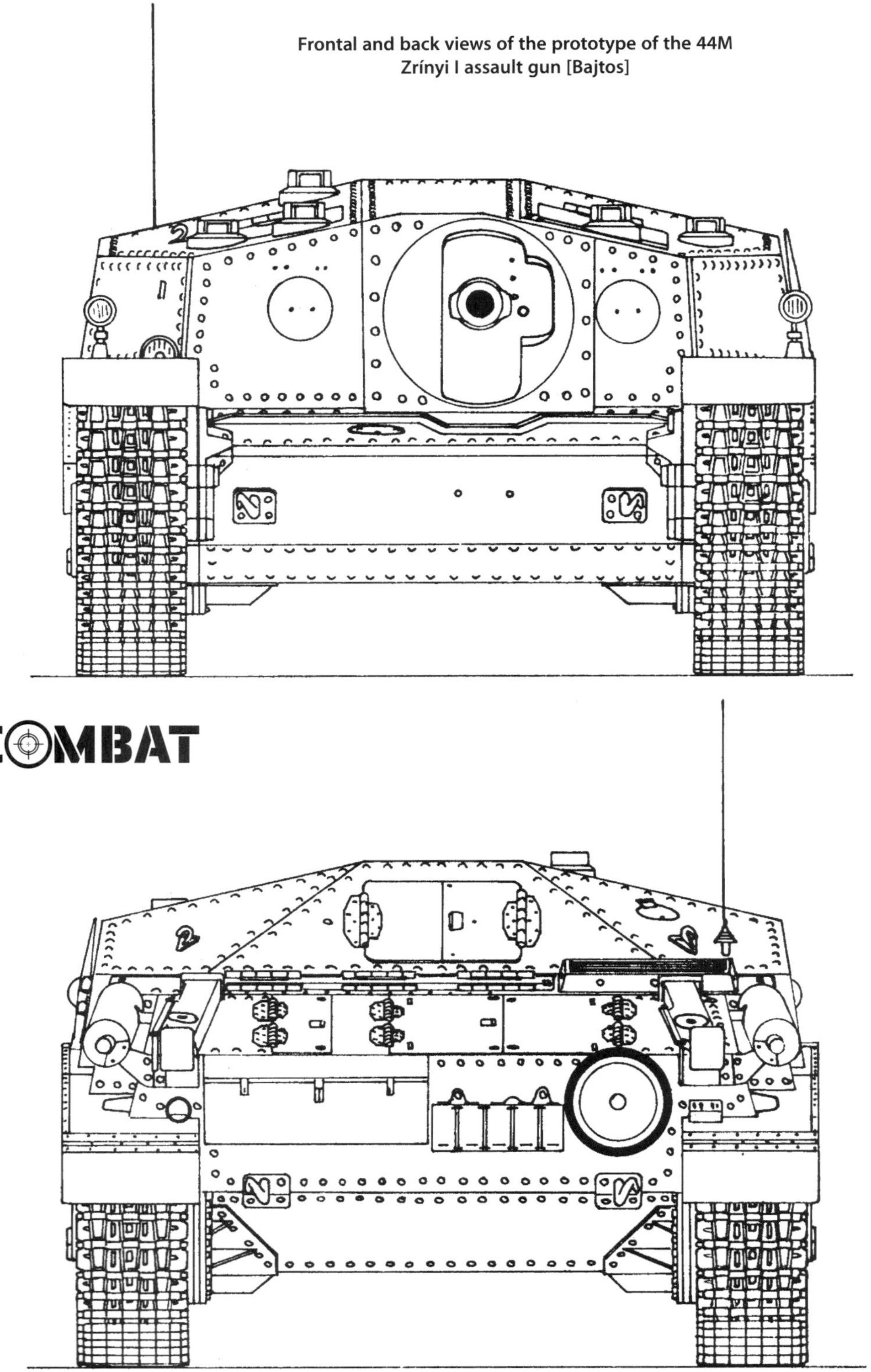

Frontal and back views of 40/43M Zrínyi II assault howitzer [Bajtos]

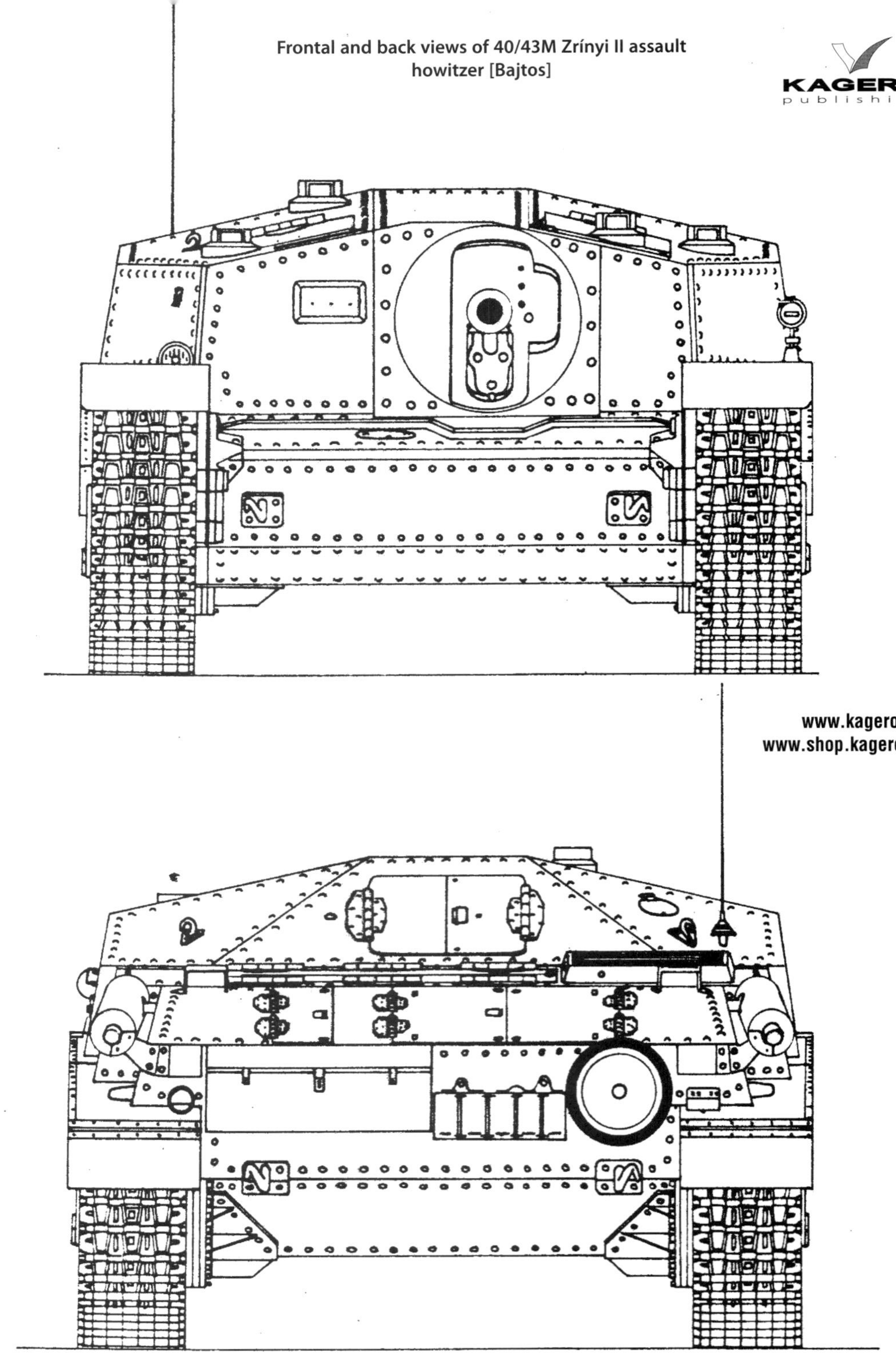

Rearview of the Zrínyi assault artillery vehicle. [Bajtos]

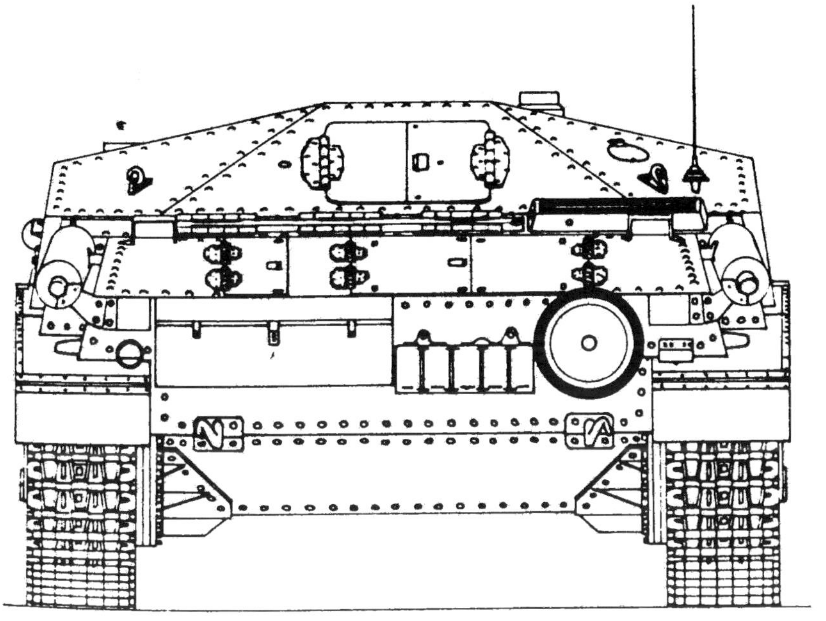

Top view of 40/43M Zrínyi II assault howitzer [Bajtos]

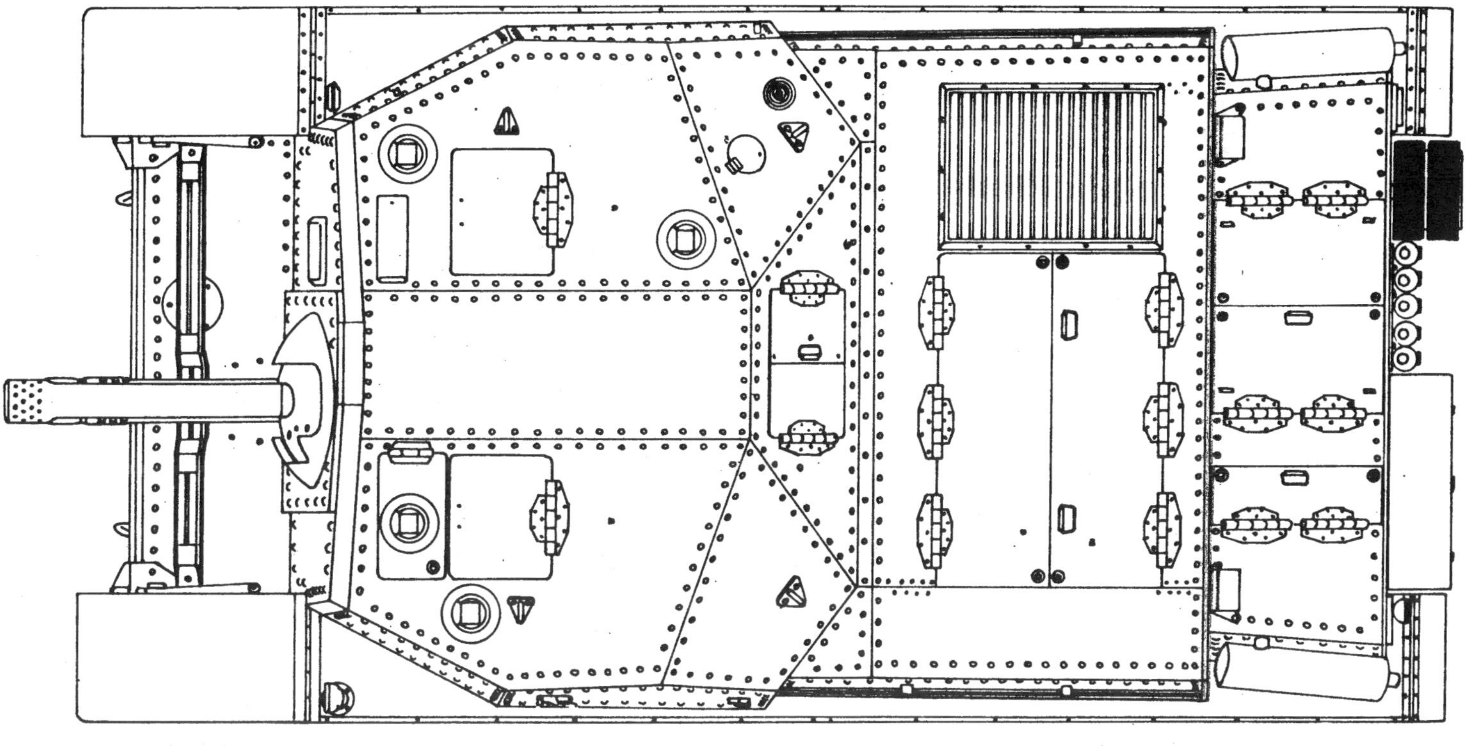

Top and side view of the 44M Zrínyi I assault gun [Bajtos]

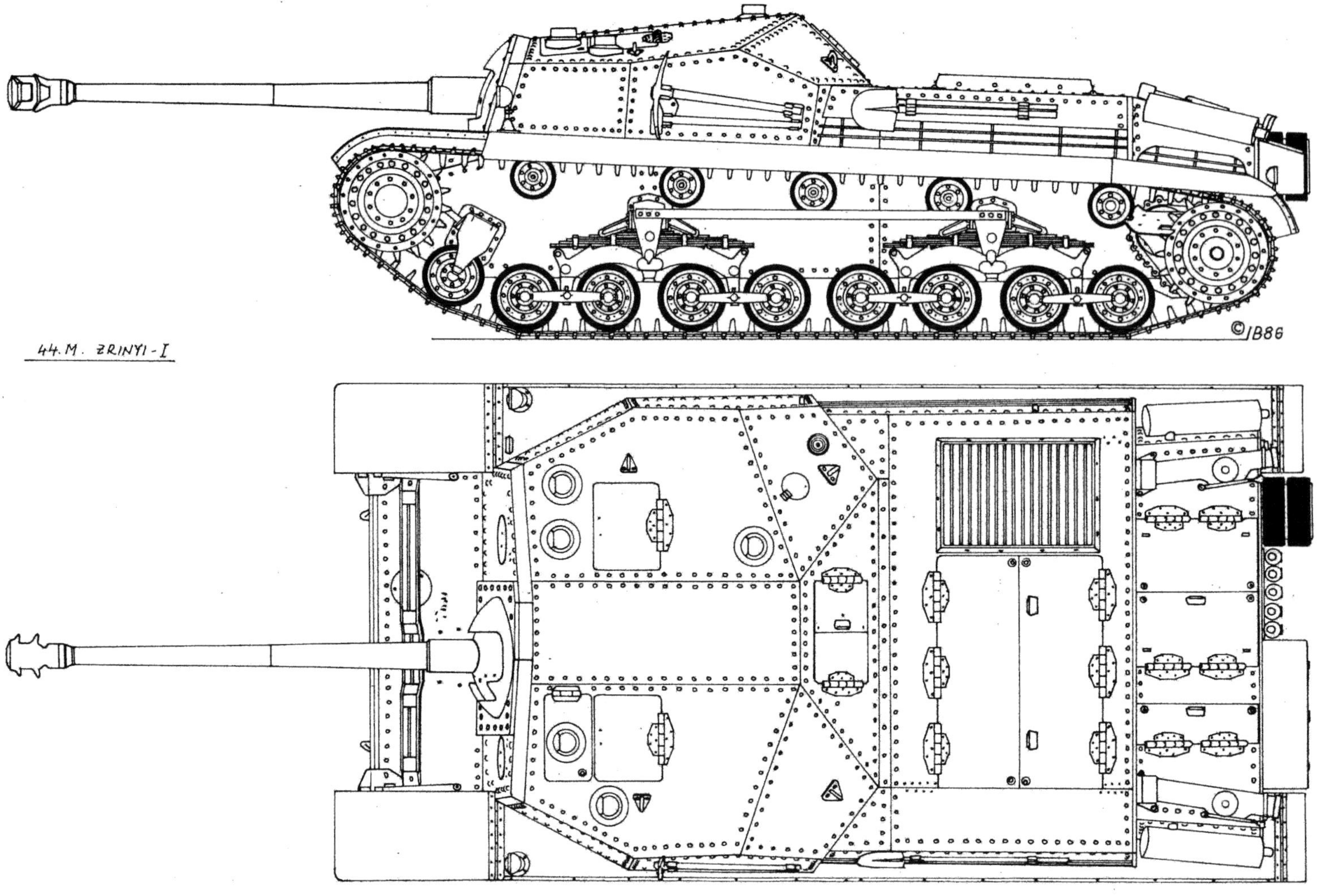

Skirt plated 40/43M Zrínyi II assault howitzer [Bajtos]

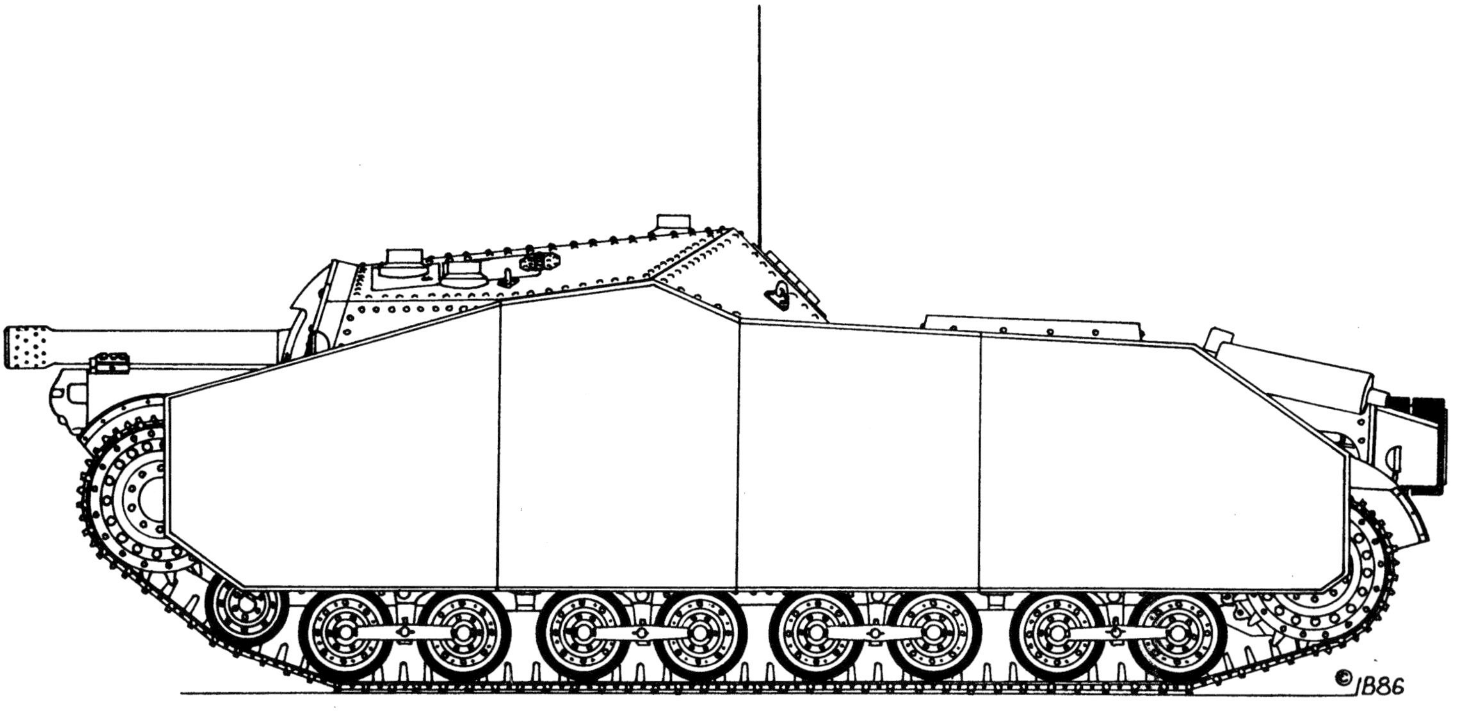

Armour protection of the Zrínyi assault artillery vehicle, the thickness of the plate given in millimetres. [Bajtos]

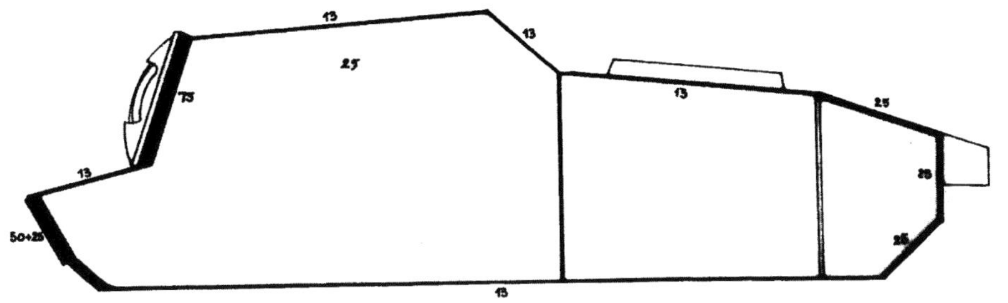

Top view of the technical drawings of the Turán tank, identical, but 400 millimetres narrower than the Zrínyi, showing the engine compartment, transmission system. [Service manual]

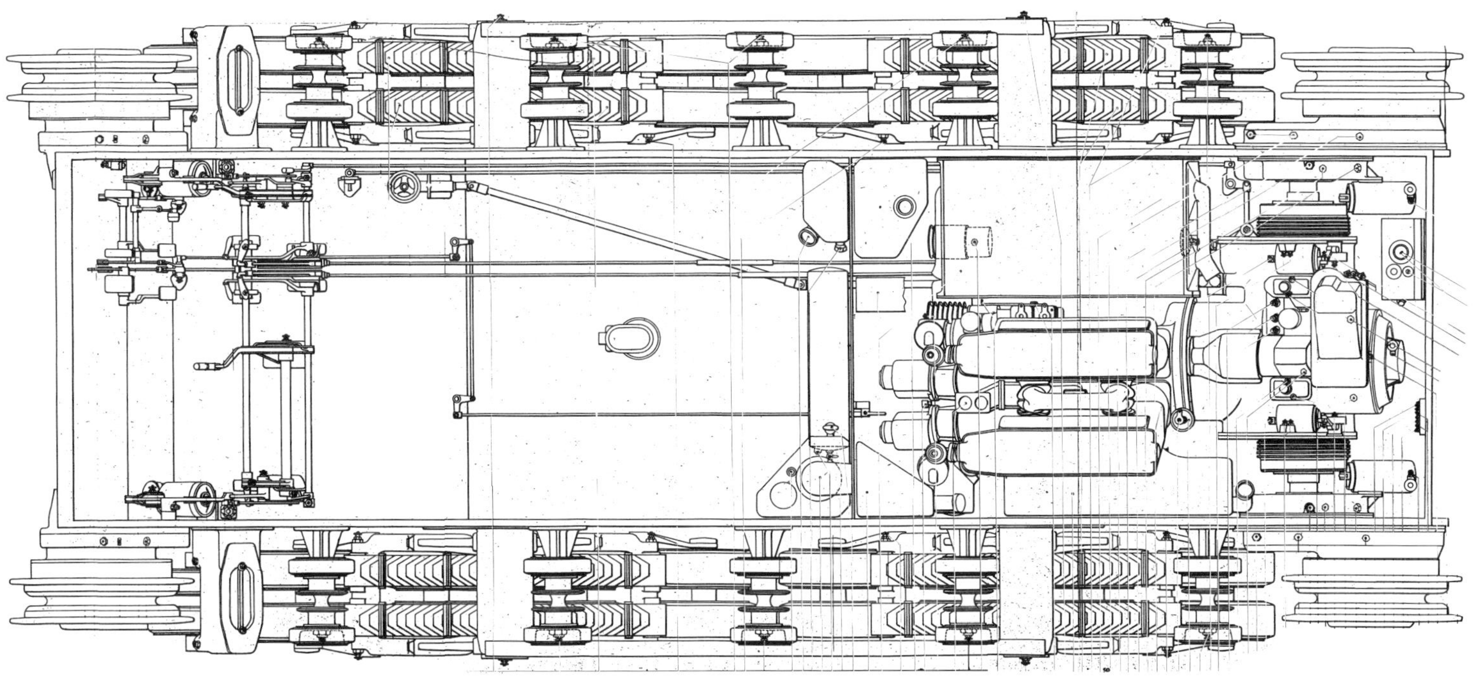

Technical side drawings of the engine compartment housing Weis Manfred V8 engine at the Zrínyi assault vehicles. [Service manual]

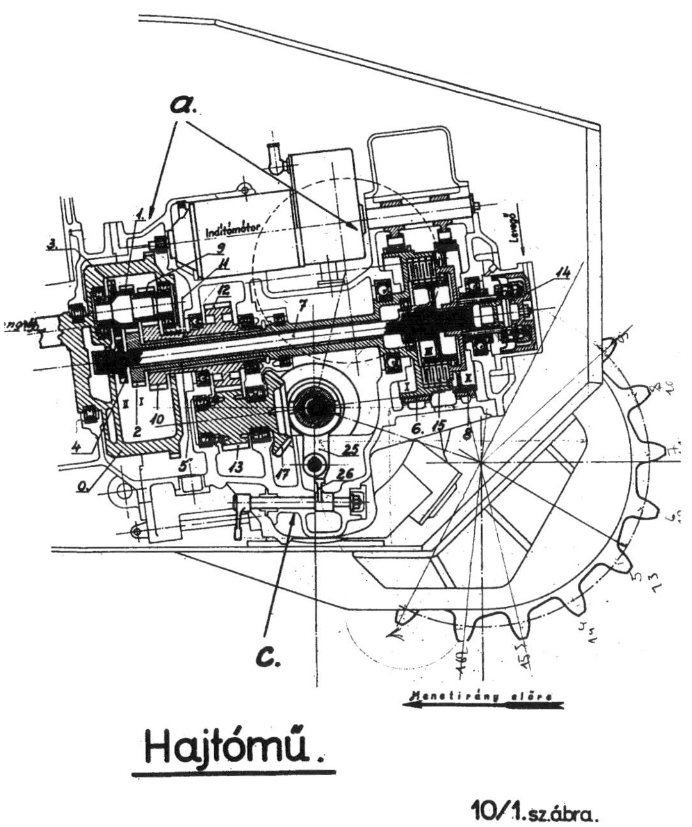

Running rollers with the leaf spring system. [Service manual]

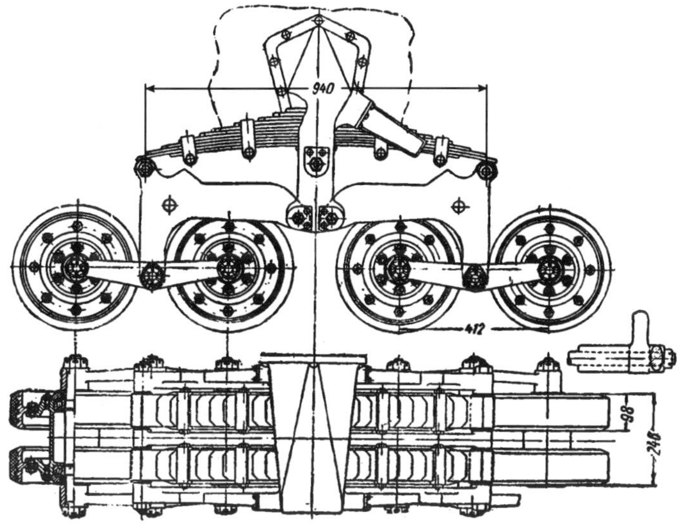

Tools attached to the inner side of the frontal mudguards, wire cutter, axe and track repair tool. [Service manual]

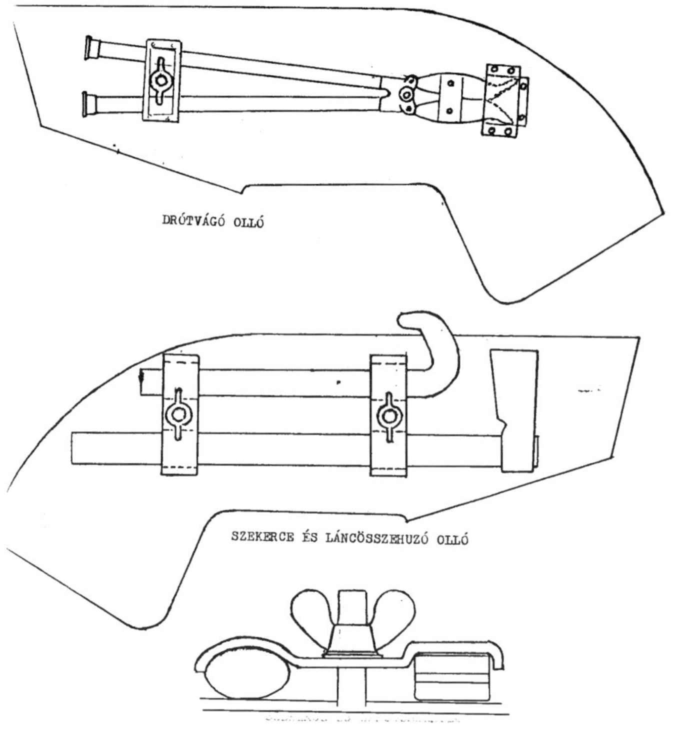

Tools, wire cutter, hammer and fire extinguisher. [Service manual]

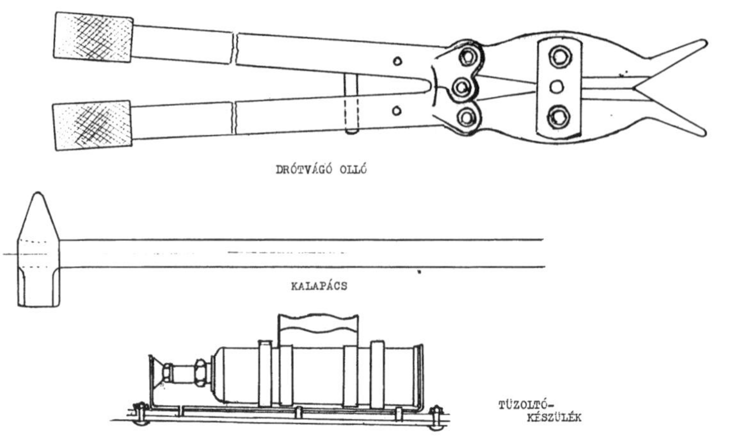

Driver's dashboard. [Service manual]

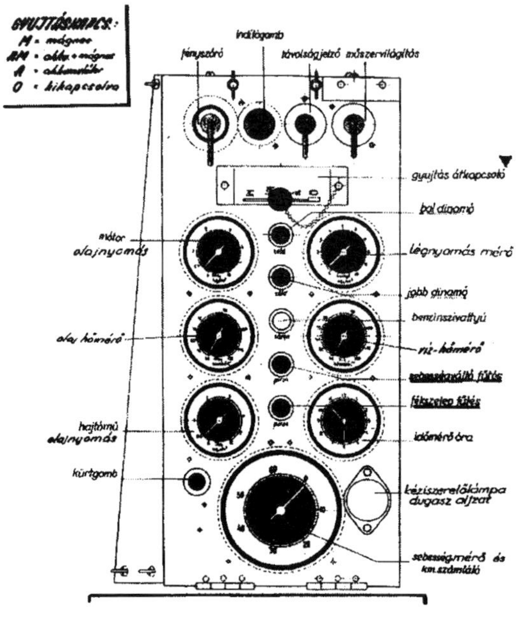

Driver's position. [Bíró]

Position of the crew, left side view, at the front of the gun layer, behind him in the centre is the commander of the vehicle at open hatches position. [Bíró]

Right side view, at the front, is the driver; behind him are the loader/radioman and commander in closed hatches position. [Bíró]

Gun cradle and firing mechanism of the 105mm 40M howitzer built into the Zrínyi II assault howitzer. [Service manual]

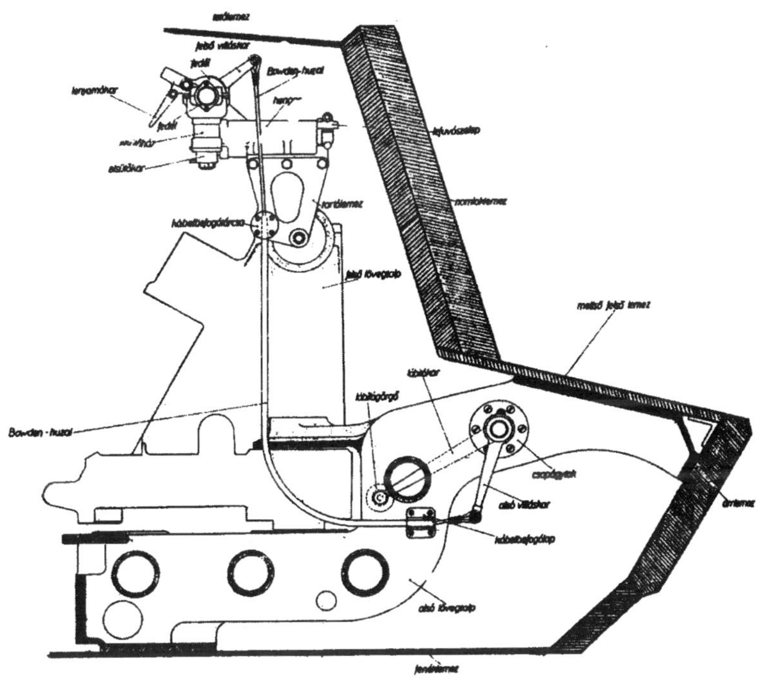

Gun cradle with the barrel of the 105mm 40M howitzer. [Service manual]

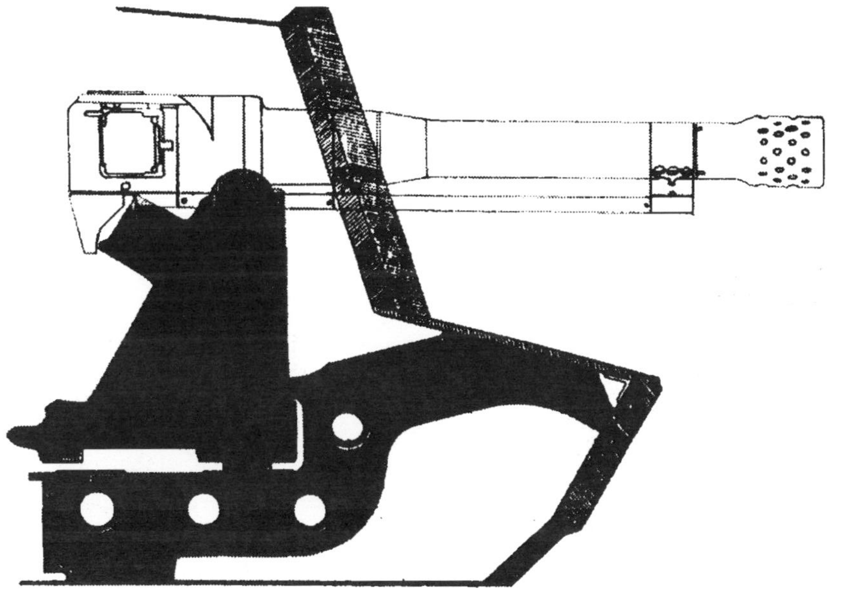

The 105mm 40M howitzer with the recoil system. [Service manual]

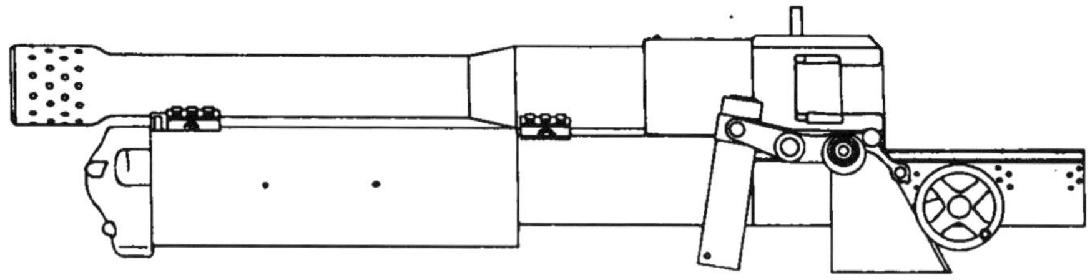

The barrel of the 105mm 40M howitzer built in the Zrínyi II assault howitzer. [Service manual]

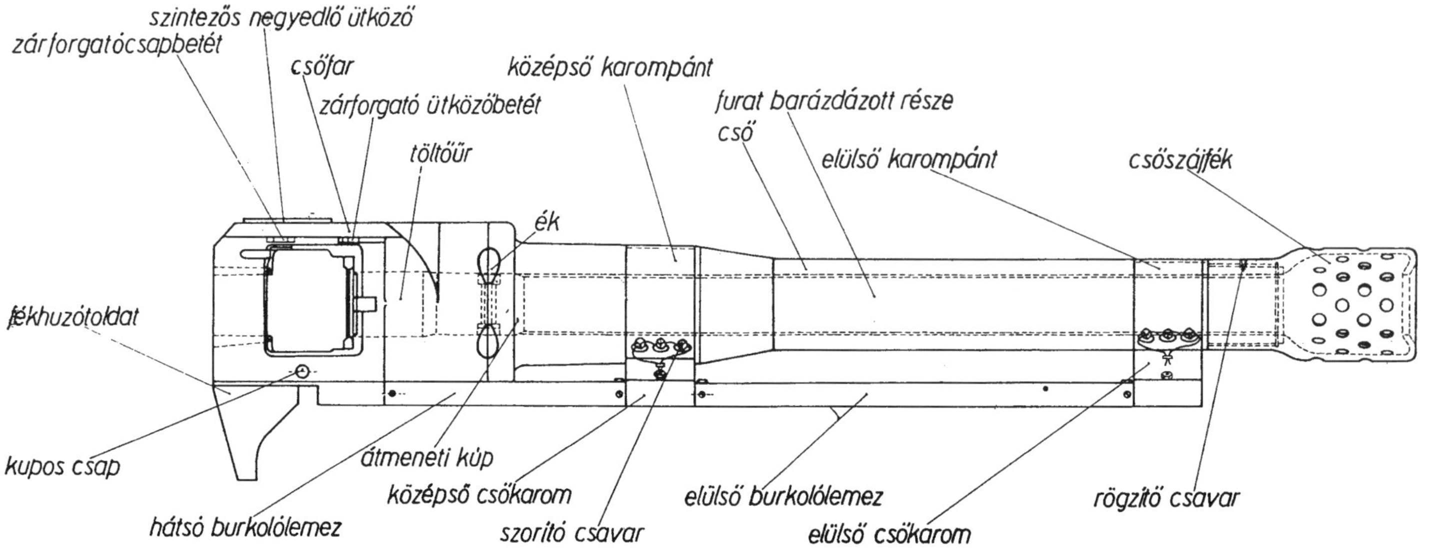

The 105mm 40M howitzer fired divided ammunitions, splinter and HE-AP shells. [Service manual]

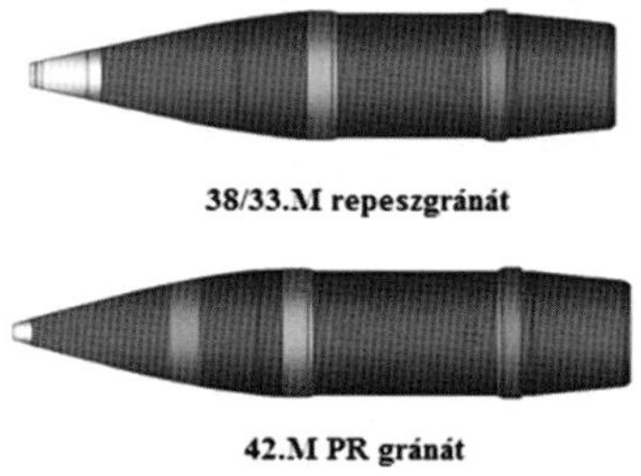

Gun layer position. [Bíró]

Side dimension and position of the howitzer inside the fighting compartment. [Bíró]

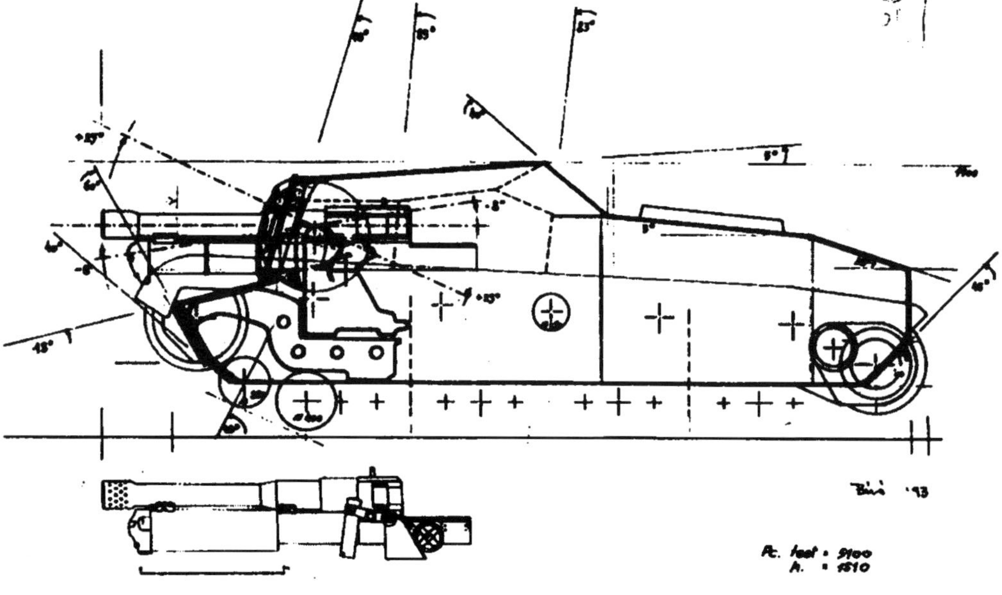

Infographical Order of Battle of the 1st Assault Artillery Battalion in 1944.

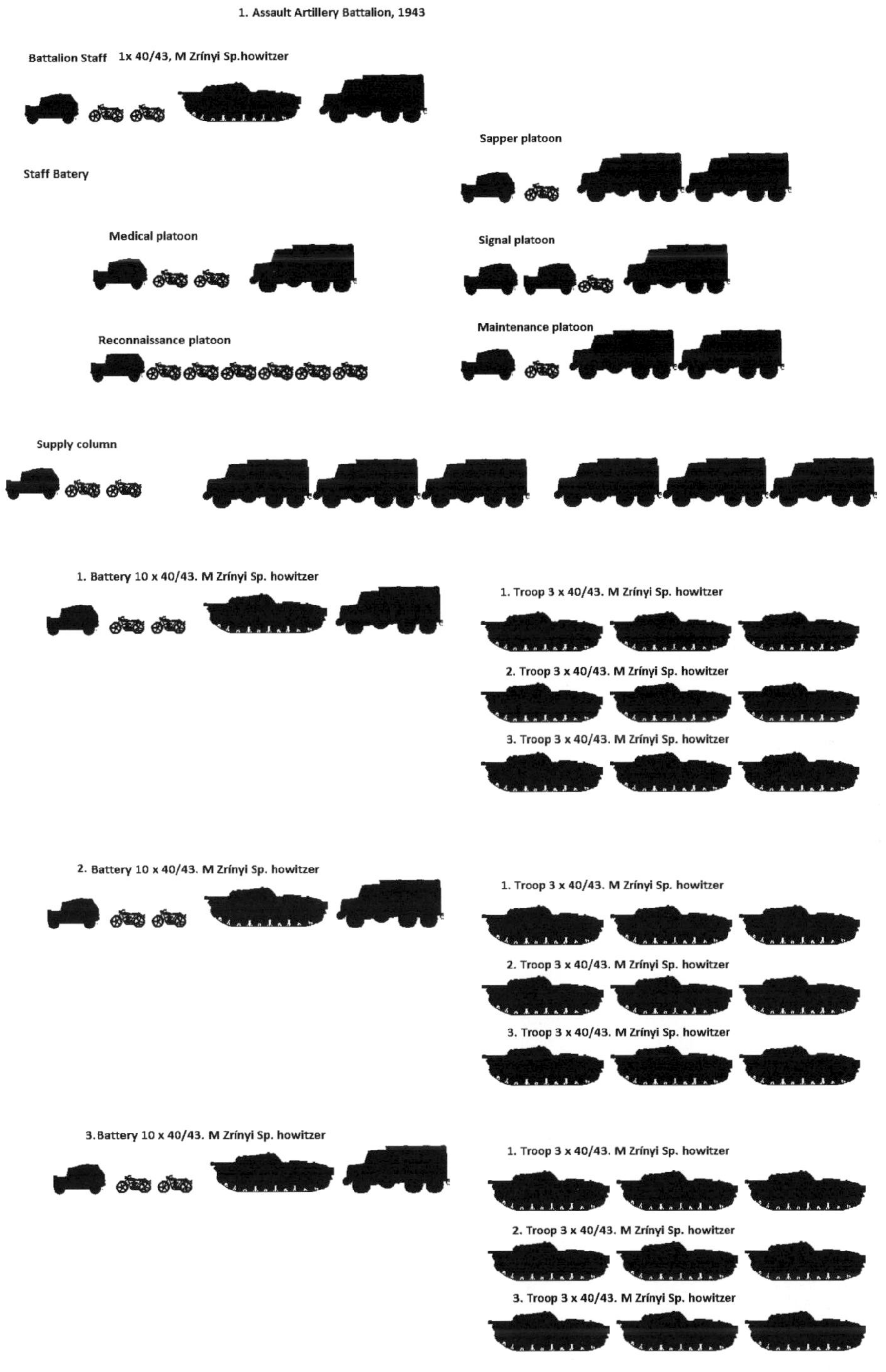

1st Lieutenant Fedór Wáczek, commander of the 1/3rd Assault Artillery Battalion briefing his men before the deployment to the Eastern Front in summer of 1944. Behind the crew, the tactical numbering of the 1/3rd Battery is visible on the vehicles. [Kovácsházy]

40/43M Zrínyi assault howitzer belonged to the 1st Battery of the 1st Assault Artillery Battalion at Stanislaw in summer of 1944. The protection was improved with side skirt plates and spare tracks attached to the hull. [Szollár]

1st Lieutenant Fedor Wáczek, commander of the 3rd Battery of the 1st Assault Artillery Battalion, first time wounded in action on 28 April 1944. [Kovácsházy]

Skirt plated 40/43M Zrínyi assault howitzer of the 1st Battery of the 1st Assault Artillery Battalion at Galicia, the large military insignia and the tactical numbers painted on the skirt. [Szollár]

– Three batteries, each with the same organization (3x10 assault guns)

- Battery commander's assault gun
- Tree troops with three assault guns in each
- Medical section
- Maintenance section
- Supply section

– Maintenance battery: to carry out the short and medium-term repair and maintenance of the weapons and armament.

– Transport battery: with heavy tractors to transport those AFVs which were unable to be towed

Hungarian infantry and the Zrínyi assault howitzers of the 3rd Battery of the 1st Assault Artillery Battalion assembling for an attack against the Soviet position in April of 1944, Galicia. [Szollár]

1st Lieutenant Tibor Rátz, commander of the 3rd Battery, Captain József Barankay, commander of the 1st Assault Artillery Battalion and 1st Lieutenant Károly Takács on 10 July 1944. 1st Lieutenant Rátz wearing custom-tailored camouflaged overalls. [Kovácsházy]

Funeral of Captain Barankay, he was killed in action on 13 July 1944 at Targovich. The battalion commander's coffin carried on his 40/43M Zrínyi assault howitzer. On the right mudguard, the battalion unit sign on the left his sign, a white card symbol was painted. [Kovácsházy]

Withdrawing vehicles of the 1st Assault Artillery Battalion at the Carpathian Mountains in summer of 1944. The skirt plates removed to move faster, the spare tracks attached to the hull. [Bonhardt]

Retreating Zrínyi of the 2nd Assault Artillery Battery of the 1st Battalion, resupply was difficult, the vehicles carried spare fuel drum, behind the assault howitzer is a 38M Botond truck visible. [Bonhardt]

40/43M Zrínyi assault howitzer of the 1st Assault Artillery Battalion captured by the Soviet Army in summer of 1944. The assault howitzer carried a personal sign, the name of "IRÉNKE" painted on the driver's visor apparatus. This vehicle currently exhibited in Kubinka, Tank Museum. [Sárhidai]

Ammunition resupply of the Zrínyi assault howitzer of 3rd Battery, 1st Assault Artillery Battalion at Galicia summer of 1944, the crew loading the divided ammunition into the vehicle. [Mujzer]

According to the original plans, the first and the second batteries should be equipped with assault guns, and the third with assault howitzers. In the practice, the organization and equipment of the Hungarian battalions remained homogenous.

The last two batteries (maintenance and transport) never materialized.

Only the 1st and the 10th Assault Artillery Battalion were equipped with Zrínyi II assault howitzers.

Resting Zrínyi assault howitzer and its crew belonged to the 1/3rd Battery at the River Bystrica at Stanislaw in summer of 1944. [Bonhardt]

40/43M Zrínyi assault howitzer was relatively small; it carries the side skirts made of four separated, perforated skirt plates per side. [Bonhardt]

Engine maintenance of the 40/43M Zrínyi assault howitzer belonged to the 1st Assault Artillery Battalion at Galicia in summer of 1944. The vehicle has spare tracks attached to the hull to improve the protection. [Deák]

Wooden bridged collapsed under the weight of the 40/43M Zrínyi assault howitzer, during the retreat in the Carpathian Mountain, jerry cans and fuel drums secured to the deck of the vehicles. [ECPA]

Knocked out Zrínyi assault howitzer of 1st Lieutenant Tibor Rátz, commander of the 1/3rd Assault Artillery Battery after the siege of Budapest, spring of 1945. [Fortepan]

Captured 41M Turán heavy tanks and 40/43M Zrínyi assault howitzers in a collection point of the Red Army, outskirt of Budapest. The mudguard of the 41M Turán has the unit sign of the 1/3rd Assault Artillery Battalion. [Bonhardt]

Another view of 1st Lieutenant Tibor Rátz's Zrínyi assault howitzer of the 1/3rd Assault Artillery Battery after the siege of Budapest, at Vérmező/ Buda side at spring of 1945. The white painted "SÁRIKA" was the fiancé's name of the 1st Lieutenant. [Fortepan]

Side view of 1st Lieutenant Tibor Rátz, Zrínyi assault howitzer with the Soviet War Trophy Collection Unit white painted serial number at Budapest, spring of 1945. [Fortepan]

The vehicle park was mixed, in the fighting echelon, 38M Rába Botonds trucks were deployed. Ammunition and equipment transported with Opel Blitz and Deutz-Klöckner trucks. Command cars were Krupp Protze and Mercedes G5, BMW R-75 sidecar, and Puch G350 solo motorcycles were used for dispatch riders and reconnaissance. The fuel was transported by two fuel tanker trucks per battery plus in "Jerry cans".

The 1st Assault Artillery Battalion was also responsible to organize and execute a second training course in Hajmáskér, which provided the staff (officers, NCO's and soldiers) of the further seven other assault artillery battalions.

The organization of the new assault artillery battalions ended on 1 April 1944 with forming the Royal Hungarian 7th, 10th, 13th, 16th, 20th, 24th, and 25th Assault Artillery Battalions beside the already existing 1st Assault Artillery Battalion.

The OB of the assault artillery battalions in theory and reality		
Subunits	**Planned OB**	**Actual OB**
Staff Battery/Battalion Staff	16 officers, 200 men	14 officers, 118 men
Maintenance Battery	6 officers, 100 men	nonexisting
Transport Battery	1 officer, 80 men	nonexisting
Assault Artillery Battery (3x)	6 officers, 110 men	5 officers, 80 men
Assault Artillery Battalion	41 officers, 710 men	29 officers, 358 men
40/43. M Zrínyi assault howitzer	31	31
Cars, trucks	120	57
Motorcycles	70	14

Camouflaged 40/43M Zrínyi assault howitzers and infantry armed with 07/31M Schwarzlose machine gun fighting at South-Transylvania in September 1944. [Kovácsházy]

Each battalion had one assault artillery cadre and one training subsection besides the depot and maintenance section in its peacetime garrison.

OPERATIONAL HISTORY OF THE ZRÍNYI ASSAULT HOWITZERS

THE 1ST ASSAULT ARTILLERY BATTALION

The 1st Assault Artillery Battalion was mobilized on 12 April 1944 to join the 1st Hungarian Army already deployed to Galicia. At the time of mobilization, only the battalion's Staff and the 2nd and 3rd Batteries had assault howitzers. The 1st Battery just got its vehicles in early June 1944 and followed the battalion to the battlefield.

1/1st Assault Artillery Battery

The 1/1st Battery arrived at Stanislau by rail transportation on June 16, 1944. At Grabitz the battery supported a Hungarian infantry battalion, but the Zrínyis ran on an unknown Hungarian minefield and two assault howitzers become unmovable. A few days later, a rescue mission was organized to recollect the lost assault howitzers from the no-man land. One of the damaged Zrínyi was successfully towed away under heavy enemy mortar fire. The other one was not recovered, made unserviceable, and left on the spot. The great Soviet attack at the end of July forced the Hungarian troops to retreat, so 1/1st Battery returned to Hajmáskér in September 1944.

1/2nd Assault Artillery Battery

The Battery arrived at Stanislau by rail transportation on 16 April. The baptism of fire of the Battery was on 21 April 1944, at Bohorodizyn. The Hungarians reconnoitered enemy anti-tank battery and an assembling infantry regiment at the edge of a nearby forest. The Zrínyi assault howitzers attacked at maximum speed on the field. The Soviet anti-tank battery was destroyed by two minutes quick burst of fire by one assault howitzer platoon. The other Zrínyi platoon performed a 5 minutes volley with fragmentation rounds against the Soviet infantry regiment. The destruction of the assault guns is well illustrated by the fact that the accompanying Hungarian infantry named the forest "deadwood" because they have never seen so much dead enemy at all.

On 13-14 July the 1/2nd Battery fought in the Targowica area, suffered a sensitive loss, 4 dead and 3 - later recovered - assault guns.

The battalion commander, founder, and organizer of the Hungarian assault artillery, Captain József Barankay was killed in an air attack at his command post on 13 July 1944. In August 1944 he was posthumously awarded the Officers' Gold Bravery Medal for his leadership during the Galicia campaign.

On July 24, the battle fought Winogradon with Soviet T-34 tanks, three of which were knocked out by the Zrínyi assault howitzers. The assault howitzers deployed in platoon size, sometimes individually to cover the withdrawing troops of the 1st Hungarian Army. The losses of the vehicles were continuous due to enemy actions, or mechanical breakdowns, lack of fuel, or getting lost in the dark.

The 1/2nd Battery arrived at Wygodar on 29 July with only three Zrínyi assault howitzers, two of them were capable to move, with unserviceable howitzers.

1/3rd Assault Artillery Battery

On 25 April 1944, the Battery received the first order to support an infantry battalion, 20 km southeast of Stanislaw Zrínyi assault howitzers knocked two out of the 8 attacking Soviet T-34s and the rest withdrew.

On 28 April 1944, the Soviets forces attacked Delatyn. 1st Lieutenant Wáczek ten Zrínyi assault howitzers attacked them out of the blue. One platoon fired, the other moved forward. The unexpected attack had a horrific impact. However, the Soviets opened fire with all short of weapons. 1st Lieutenant

Camouflaged 40/43M Zrínyi assault howitzer of the 10/2nd Assault Artillery Battery in ambush position at Torda, 22 September 1944. [Bonhard]

Wáczek, in a half-emerged position, started to observe the Soviets when he was hit. The command of the attack was taken over by Captain József Barankay, who walked among the assault howitzers during charge. The seriously injured commander was replaced by 1. Lt Tibor Rátz.

Staff Battery

On July 13, Targovich Captain József Barankay killed in action during an enemy air raid, the 1st Assault Artillery Battalion was taken over by the senior officer Captain Béla Guthy and then by Major Nándor Doóry. After that Captain Béla Guthy was seriously injured and Major Nándor Doóry got a nervous breakdown, 1st Lieutenant Dénes Sándor was appointed as the commander.

By the end of July, the Soviet attack pushed back the Hungarian troops from Galicia to the Carpathians. During the retreat, two-thirds of the assault howitzers of the 1st Assault Artillery Battalion were lost. To replace the 1st Assault Artillery Battalion in need of rest, the 10th Assault Artillery Battalion in Szigetvár was mobilized in August 1944.

Attacking 40/43M Zrínyi assault howitzer troop belonged to the 10th Assault Artillery Battalion, the other unit equipped with Zrínyi assault howitzers in 1944. [Bonhardt]

Resting crew of the 40/43M Zrínyi assault howitzer and 41m Turán heavy tank during the short lull of the fighting in September 1944, South-Transylvania. [Bonhardt]

Field repair of a damaged 40/43M Zrínyi assault howitzer belonged to the 10th assault Artillery Battalion, on the road between Kolozsvár and Torda, September 1944. [Bonhardt]

THE 10TH ASSAULT ARTILLERY BATTALION

The battalion was formed in March 1944. As a result of the death of the legendary commander of the 1st Assault Artillery Battalion, Captain Alexander Sándor Hanák took over the 10th Assault Artillery Battalion, and its former commander Major Nándor Doóri, was posted to commanding the 1st Assault Artillery Battalion.

The 10th Assault Artillery Battalion was filled up to 65% when the Romanians left the alliance of the Axis powers in mid-August 1944. Two batteries of the battalion were immediately mobilized and deployed by train from Dombóvár, as long as the ongoing military operation allowed the transportation by rail. On 28 August 1944, the troops disembarked at Csíkszentsimon. The task of the deployed assault artillery unit was primarily to show force and support of the weak Hungarian border guard troops. The Staff Battery, the 1st and 2nd Batteries were baptized in fire at the Uz Valley and Szépvíz on 20 September 1944. The first 40/43M Zrínyi assault howitzer was lost here.

Due to the advance of the enemy, the 10th Assault Artillery Battalion withdrew at the end of September, along the way of Gyergyószentmiklós – Maroshévíz – Déda – Kolozsvár (Gheorgheni - Maroshévíz - Deda - Cluj – Napoca). The 1st and 2nd Batteries were in action alternately around the battles of Torda.

On 22 September 1944, a Soviet attack emerged in the direction of Sósfürdő, on a narrow space with two Soviet rifle divisions supported by fifty T-34 tanks. At Egerbegy, the 4th Soviet Guard Division attacked, on the left side supported by Romanian troops. The battled parts of the Hungarian 2nd Armored Division resisted stubbornly.

During that afternoon, the 1/I Hungarian Infantry Battalion, reinforced by the 2nd Battery of the 10th Assault Gun Battalion ambushed the advancing Red Army troops. Six Zrínyi assault howitzers led by Ensign János Bozsoki were in the position to counter the Soviet tanks. The tasks of the Zrínyi assault howitzers were to stop the Soviet attack in the way to the Sósfürdő. The assault howitzers went into firing position at the Sósfürdő valley in front of the road leading to the enemy, halfway through 400 m. The bushy, heavily covered terrain was a great help to camouflage the assault howitzers. The advancing tanks were allowed so close, as far as it could be, 50 meters away. The well-trained crew started quick firing and in a few moments, there was nothing visible about the dust and smoke cloud caused by many impacts, which blocked the enemy to find their targets, when opening fire. After about 3-4 minutes of fire, Ensign Bozsoki ordered a ceasefire. The steep shore of the deep-cut road half-buried the spilled and smashed T-34s. The Hungarian assault howitzers knocked out 18 T-34 within a few minutes.

The Ensign carried out a patrol with his vehicle, leaving the rest of his unit behind at Sósfürdő. Upon hearing

Artillery Ensign János Bozsóki served with the 10th Assault Artillery Battalion, decorated for bravery at Torda on 22 September, when his battery knocked out 18 Soviet T-34 tanks. [Illésfalvi]

Heavily camouflaged 40/43M Zrínyi assault howitzer with its distinctive perforated muzzle brake of the 105mm howitzer. [Deák]

Zrínyi assault howitzer of the 10th Assault Artillery Battalion slipped into a ditch during the retreat in September 1944. The infantryman on the right had a German-style metal gas mask carrier. [Illésfalvi]

the sound of battle behind him, he returned to find his men dead or wounded following another Soviet attack, and three Zrínyis were immobile. Ensign Bozsoki led the two serviceable vehicles back to the Hungarian lines and later organized and led a recovery operation to the three damaged assault howitzers from the battlefield. For his bravery in action, Ensign János Bozsoki received the highest Hungarian military decoration, the Officers' Gold Bravery Medal, becoming only the seventh Hungarian officer to earn this medal during the war.

Parallel to the Torda deployment, in the area of Arad (Oradea), between Magyarcséke, Drágcsék, and Tőkefalva, the 10/3rd Battery was deployed.

In December 1944, the remaining assault howitzers of the battalion were transported to Székesfehérvár via Budapest.

On 7 December 1944, with the 271st German Volks Division, the 10th Assault Artillery Battalion was assigned to the task of blocking the advancing enemy from the Ercsi bridgehead towards to Rácszentpéter, which enemy advance could threaten the road between Budapest-Székesfehérvár. The counterattack was carried out by the 10/3rd and 1/3rd Battery (which joined to the attack later on). Together 11 assaults howitzer took part in the action with infantry to cover them (with Hungarian and German accompanying infantry) in Martonvásár - Rácszentpéter district. As a result of the impetuous attack of the Zrínyi assault howitzers, the Soviets began to escape and left a significant number of weapons and transport vehicles behind.

According to Captain Sándor Hanák's decision, under his leadership, the 1st Battery with 11 Zrínyi assault howitzers continues the fight in the defense of Budapest under the command of Major General Ernő Billnitzer (commander of the Assault Artillery Branch). The rest of the battalion, lack of assault artillery vehicles moved to Mosonszolnok, hoping retraining and assault guns under the command of 1st Lieutenant Dénes Mikéta.

ZRÍNYI ASSAULT HOWITZERS DURING THE SIEGE OF BUDAPEST 1944-1945

Six assault gun battalions, led by Lieutenant General Ernő Billnitzer, commander of assault artillery troops, had 2000 men with 30 assault guns and 8 anti-tank guns. The battalions were equipped with Zrínyis, StuGs. However, the majority of the trained crews were deployed as infantry. The assault guns provided a formidable threat to the advancing Russian troops. The size and armament of the Zrínyis were ideal for street fighting. Their low silhouette helped to conceal them, and the l05mm howitzer could penetrate any Russian armor at close range.

During the siege of Budapest, the 1st, 7th (StuG III), 10th, and parts of the 13th, 16th, 25th Assault Artillery Battalions fought in the city. The units were reinforced with freshly assembled Zrínyis from the Ganz factory.

The 7th Assault Gun Battalion had four-five StuG.III self-propelled guns. The 10/1st Assault Artillery Battery had eleven Zrínyi assault howitzers and 50 trucks commanded by 1st Lt. Dénes Csáth.

The 1/1st Assault Artillery Battery was armed with heavy infantry weapons (light and heavy machine guns). 2nd Battery

Children posing on a blown-up 40/43M Zrínyi assault howitzer at Kelenföld/Buda after the siege of Budapest in summer of 1945. [Bonhardt]

Romanian troops riding on a captured Hungarian 40/43M Zrínyi assault howitzer advancing trough a captured Transylvanian town in autumn of 1944. The Zrínyi could be identified by the single spare roller next to the smoke candles and the toolbox. [Mujzer]

was partially and the 3rd Battery was filled with Zrínyi assault howitzers.

Due to the seriousness of the situation, since the middle of November, the Hungarian assault howitzers were subordinated to various German and Hungarian military commanders and were deployed in piece mail fashion in the areas of Maglód, Ecser, Pécel, and Érd (around Budapest).

On 3 November 1944, the 1/3rd Battery with three Zrínyi assault howitzers attacked the Soviet forces near Ferihegy Airport and pursuing them to Vecsés while causing heavy losses to them. On the next day, the 3rd Battery knocked out four of the six Soviet tank T-34s attacking at Vecsés.

Sunday 5 November 1944, the troops of the 8th SS Cavalry Division supported by the composite force of the 1st and 10th Assault Artillery Battalions launched an attack on Soviet forces that embedded at the southern part of Vecsés that day and soon expelled most of them.

The battalion commander of the 1st Assault Artillery Battalion, Captain Wáczek Fedor, on 19 November 1944 near Maglód was again seriously wounded during a reconnaissance. The command was taken over by 1st Lieutenant Dénes Sándor.

From 25 to 28 December, the Soviet troops occupied Albertfalva and the Kelenföld Railway Station. Three assault howitzers of the 1/3rd Battery supported the German-Hungarian troops on 27 December recaptured the railway station. The street fighting in Budapest started after the encirclement of 24 December 1944 in various parts of the city. The maintenance workshop was located in Pest in Danube Vigadó's Dance Hall.

War trophy collection point at Budapest in spring of 1945, Turán, Zrínyi, Italian M15, Grille, Pz. III and Matilda armoured vehicles can be seen with the Soviet War Trophy Collection Unit's numbers painted on the vehicles.

War Trophy Exhibition at River Néva, Moscow, summer of 1945, on the left the nose of the Zrínyi is visible.

War Trophy Exhibition at River Néva, Moscow, summer of 1945, on the left is the 40M Nimród self-propelled autocannon, on the right is the back of the Zrínyi is visible.

With the diminished number of Zrínyis, the assault howitzers had to go to action every day. Due to the losses, the crew has changed constantly. It was no longer the original crew's position; everybody had to perform in every position. Only the mechanics were not assigned to a combat task. They were essential to keep moving the Zrínyi assault howitzers.

On 10 January 1945, the 10th Assault Artillery Battalion reinforced with the 1/3rd Battery numbering ten assault howitzers supported by 150-200 men strong German-Hungarian combat team assembled behind the current MTK football field. The Zrínyis overrun the fence and fired the drunken Soviet infantry seated at the stage of the football stadium with fragmentations shots, leaving about 800 dead Red Army men after the attack.

On 12 January, three Zrínyi assault howitzers of the 10/1st Battery fought a serious battle with the Soviet tanks in the barracks of Maria Theresia of Üllői Road. During the clash, János Bozsoki, battery commander was injured and one Zrínyi was knocked out by the Soviets.

On 26 January 1945 four-five assault howitzers of the 1/3rd and 10/1st Batteries with the support of German armored personal carriers launched an attack at Daróci Road, on the Army Central Uniform Depot. The attack was unsuccessful, the enemy re-occupied the building.

The next day, one Zrínyi assault howitzer under the command of officer candidate sergeant Péter Városy and one German armored personal carrier with a flamethrower carried out fire strikes which forced the Soviets out of the building.

On 9 February 1945, the last, four serviceable assault howitzers of 1/3rd Battery (also the last serviceable assault howitzers of the 1st Assault Artillery Battalion), fired their last HE shots towards the enemy.

CAMOUFLAGE AND MARKINGS

CAMOUFLAGE

Until 1942, this disruptive camouflage was brush-applied with hard-edged patterns of irregular blotches. However, in 1942 the Hungarians began to use spray equipment on the Turáns and other types, giving the camouflage patterns a more diaphanous appearance. An army regulation defined the camouflage colors to be used, but the style of the patches varied according to the different factories where the vehicles were produced. The Zrínyi assault howitzers were delivered in dark olive-green paint to the troops, later three-tone camouflage was applied on them. The skirt plates were also painted in three-tone camouflage.

MILITARY INSIGNIA

The order issued on the 16 of November 1942 prohibited the use of the old insignia and introduced a new, uniform one, already used by the air force - white cross over a black square – authorized in three different sizes according to the location on the vehicles. The instructions required the insignia to be placed on all visible sides of vehicles, but in practice, it was applied only to the flanks and in increased size to the engine deck. Later of course there were occasions when the required dimensions of the insignia were visibly changed, e.g. on the Zrinyi assault-howitzers of the 1st Assault Artillery Battalion. Some reminiscences recall that on occasions only the white cross was applied without the black square.

UNIT SIGNS

Standard requirements were to use adaptations of easy geometrical symbols. The regulations forbade the use of the Hun-

40/43M Zrínyi assault howitzer at Kubinka in the early 70s, the spare tracks and mudguards removed, the side skirts on. [Sárhidai]

garian crown, wings, or the death's head in a unit insignia. The crown was part of the national insignia, the air force used the wings, and the death's head belonged to the chemical warfare units. Nevertheless, almost all unit insignia incorporated at least one of these symbols. The 1st Assault Artillery Battalion had the white skull crossed barrel insignia. In 1944 the 1st Assault Artillery Battalion sign was painted on the left and right front and rear hull or mud-guards. The non-armored vehicles also carried unit signs, following the above-mentioned regulations.

LICENSE PLATES

On the armored vehicles, the front serial number was shown in a thin white rectangle. The style was usually an H, with the national shield (red-white-green), followed by a three-digit serial number. The capital H referred to the Honvéd (Hungarian Army). The H and the numbers were painted in black. The same serial numbers were on the rear of the hull but in a square shape. Later, from 1944, the front license plate was simply painted on the camouflage without the white rectangle. On each license plate, the numbers identified the type of vehicle: 1 H identified the Turán 40M, 2H was the Turán 41M, and 3H was the Zrínyi.

TACTICAL NUMBERING

In 1944 the armored division used a four-digit tactical number painted only on the rear plate of the turret. The Zrínyi assault gun battalions used different tactical numbers. Sometimes they showed the battalion and the battery number, e.g. 1+1, which meant the 1st Battery of the 1st Assault Gun Battalion, with the military insignia in the middle. In other cases, they indicated the battery number and the individual vehicle number, e.g. 2+2 or + 36.

INDIVIDUAL MARKINGS

Individual markings were not typical among the Hungarian armored troops. It was not regulated but was tolerated by the Army during the war. Nevertheless, at the end of the war, some assault guns were found to have individual markings. The most well-known example was a knocked-out Zrínyi in Budapest, 1945, which after the siege was found with the inscription "SÁRIKA" visible on the observation port on the driver's side. The vehicle belonged to the 1/3rd Battery and was the personal vehicle of the battery commander, 1st Lieutenant Tibor Rátz. Another example is the 40/43M Zrínyi assault howitzer captured by the Soviet Army in summer of 1944 at Galicia, belonged to the 1st Assault Artillery Battalion with the name of "IRÉNKE" painted on the driver's visor apparatus.

BIBLIOGRAPHY

A m. kir. Fegyveres erők képeskrónikája (1919-1945), Vitézi Szék, 1977
Az elsodort város, Emlékkötet a Budapestért folytatott harcok 60. évfordulójára 1944-45, PolgART, 2005
„Álltak Tordánál a csatát fejtőig vérben", Emlékkönyv a tordai csata 60. évfordulójára, 2004 Torda
Balla Tibor – Csikány Tamás – Gulyás Géza – Horváth Csaba – Kovács Vilmos: A
Bíró Ádám – Éder Miklós – Sárhidai Gyula: A magyar királyi honvédség külföldi gyártású páncélos harcjárművei 1920- 1945, Petit Real, 2006
Bíró Ádám – Éder Miklós – Sárhidai Gyula: A magyar királyi honvédség hazai gyártású páncélos harcjárművei 1920- 1945, Petit Real, 2012
Bonhardt Attila: Zrínyi II rohamtarack, Pekó Kiadó 2015
Bonhardt Attila – Sárhidai Gyula – Winkler Róbert: A magyar királyi honvédség fegyverzete 1919-45 part 1, Zrínyi, 1992
Bús János- Szabó Péter: Béke poraikra, VARIETAS'93, 1999
Bús János- Szabó Péter: Béke poraikra II.. VARIETAS'93, 2001
Dombrády Loránd: A magyar gazdaság és a hadfelszerelés, 1938/44, Akadémia, 1981

Csima János: Források a Magyar Honvédség II. világháborús történetének tanulmányozásához, Zrínyi, 1961
Hajdú Ferenc – Sárhidai Gyula: A magyar királyi honvéd Haditechnikai Intézettől a HM Technológiai Hivatalig, HM Technológiai Hivatal 2005
Hingyi lászló: Budapest ostroma 1944-45, Etalon Kiadó 2018
Illésfalvi Péter – Szabó Péter – Számvéber Norbert: Erdély a Hadak Útján 1940-1944, Puedlo
Illésfalvi Péter – Kovács Vilmos – Maruzs Roland: Vitézségért, HK Hermanos, 2011
Magyarország a II. világháborúban, Enciklopédia, PETIT REAL, 1997
Maruzs Roland: Középkereszt, tisztikereszt, lovagkereszt, Zrínyi, 2013
Kamen Nevenkin: Bécs még várhat, A budapesti hadművelet bevezető szakasza, Pekó Kiadó 2014
Ölvedi Ignác: Az 1. Magyar Hadsereg története 1944. január 6.-tól október 17.-ig, Zrínyi, 1989
Számvéber Norbert: Az alföldi páncélos csata, Puedlo
Számvéber Norbert: Páncélos hadviselés a budapesti csatában, Puedlo
Számvéber Norbert: Páncélosok a Felvidéken, Puedlo
Számvébert Norbert: Páncélosok a Dunántúlon, Akadémia kiadó 2017
Szabó Péter – Számvéber Norbert: Magyarország és a keleti hadszíntér 1943-1945, Puedlo
Rada Tibor: A magyar királyi honvéd Ludovika Akadémia és testvérintézetek összefoglaló története 1930-1945, GÁLOS NYOMDÁSZ Bt, 1998
Stark Tamás: Hadak Útján, Corvina, 1991
Ungváry Krisztián: Budapest ostroma, Corvina, 1998
Ungváry Krisztián: A magyar honvédség a második világháborúban, Osiris, 2005
Veress D. Csaba: A Dunántúl hadi krónikája 1944/45, Zrínyi, 1984
Veress D. Csaba: Balatoni Csata 1944/45, Veszprém Megyei kiadványok, 1977
Veress D. Csaba: Magyarország hadikrónikája 1944-1945 I.-II. Militaria 2002

Articles

ZMKA Akadémiai Közlemények:

Jakus János: A magyar királyi 3. hadsereg megalakulása és hadműveletei (1944. szeptember-október), 1994/204

Hadtörténeti Közlemények:

Jakus János: A Magyar 3. Hadsereg harcai 1944. szeptember 22- november 3. között, HK 1995/1
Jakus János: A m. kir. IV. hadtest támadó hadműveletei 1944 szeptemberében, HK 1994/1

Haditechnikai Szemle:

Bíró Ádám: A 40/43M Zrínyi rohamtarack kifejlesztése és használata, 3. rész, 1996/4
Bíró Ádám: A 40/43M Zrínyi rohamtarack kifejlesztése és alkalmazása, 2. rész, 1996/2
Bíró Ádám: A 40/43M Zrínyi rohamtarack kifejlesztése és alkalmazása, I. rész, 1996/1
Bíró Ádám: A 40M Nimród páncélvadász- önjáró légvédelmi gépágyú, 2.rész, 1994/3
Dr. Kovács Miklós: vitéz, nemes barankai Barankay József hivatásos százados, a Magyar Tiszti Arany Vitézségi Érem kitüntetetje, 2013/6
Kovácsházi Miklós: A Zrínyi jármű család történte 1., 2013/6
Kovácsházi Miklós: A Zrínyi jármű család történte 2., 2014/1
Dr. Mujzer Péter: A Magyar Királyi honvédség páncélos csapatainak végső szervetete 1942-1944, 2016/4
Dr. Mujzer Péter: A 2. páncéloshadosztály hadműveletei Galiciában 1944-ben, I. rész, 2017/6
Dr. Mujzer Péter: A 2. páncéloshadosztály hadműveletei Galiciában 1944-ben, II. rész, 2018/1
Schmidt László: A magyar rohamtüzérség német harcjárművei, 2013/6o

Belvedere

GALLó Krisztián: Páncélosok a Kárpátokban, 2003/XV. 1-2, 3-4., 5-6.

Militaria Modell:

Éder Miklós: Magyar páncélos járművek alakulat jelzései, 1. rész, 1991 / 1
Éder Miklós: Magyar páncélos járművek alakulat jelzései, 2. rész, 1991/2
Éder Miklós: Magyar páncélosok hadi jelzése, 1917-1945, 1992/6

Pro Modell

Mujzer Péter: A magyar királyi honvédség páncélos csapatainak jelzésrendszere, 2003/1-3

Batailles&Blindes

András Palásthy: Bapteme du feu mortel en Ukraine, Batailles&Blindes n.42

Steel Masters

Les blindes de l'Axe, Steel Masters n.8, 2010

Foreign Books

Max Axworthy: Third Axis Fourth Ally, Arms and Armour, 1995
Dr Tamás Baczoni – Dr László Tóth: Hungarian Army Uniforms 1939 – 1945, HUNIFORM 2010
Csaba Becze: Magyar steel, Mashroom Publication, 2006
Dénes Bernád, Charles K. Kliment: Magyar Warriors, The history of the Royal Hungarian Armed Forces 1919-1945, volume 1, Helion Publication, 2015
Dénes Bernád, Charles K. Kliment: Magyar Warriors, The history of the Royal Hungarian Armed Forces 1919-1945, volume 2, Helion Publication, 2017
Peter Gosztonyi: Deutschlands waffengefahrten an de rost front 1941-1941, Motorbuch Verlag, 1981
Charles Kliment- Vladimir Francev: Czechoslovakian AFVs 1918-1948, Schiffer, 1997
Maksim Kolomiets – Ilia Mosanskij: Trofei v Krasnoj Armij 1941-1945, Frontovaja Illustracija 1999
Eduardo Gil Martinez: Fuerzas Acorazadas Húngaras 1939-43, Almena 2017
Perry Moore: Panzerschlacht, Armored operations on the Hungarian plains September-November, Helion, 2008
Péter Mujzer: Hungarian Mobile Forces 1920-45, Bayside Books, 2000
Péter Mujzer: Huns on Wheels, Hungarian Mobile Forces in WWII, Armoured, Cavalry, Bicycle Troops, Motorised Rifle, Mujzer and Partners Ltd., 2015
Péter Mujzer: Hungarian Armoured Forces in WWII, KAGERO Books, PHOTOSNIPER 26., 2017
Leo Niehorster: The Royal Hungarian Army 1920-45, Bayside Books, 1998
Nigel Thomas- László Pál Szabó: The Royal Hungarian Army in World War II, Ospery, 2008
Anthony Tucker-Jones: Armored warfare and Hitler's allies 1941-1945, Pen&Sword, 2013
Steven Zaloga- James Grandsen: The Eastern Front, Arms, and Armour, 1983
Steven Zaloga: Tanks of Hitler's eastern allies 1941-45, Osprey, 2013